Solomon SAYS

—

DIRECTIVES FOR
YOUNG MEN

—

MARK HORNE

ATHANASIUS
PRESS
WEST MONROE, LOUISIANA

Solomon Says
Directives for Young Men from Proverbs
Copyright © 2020 Mark Horne

Athanasius Press
715 Cypress Street
West Monroe, Louisiana 71291
www.athanasiuspress.org

Cover design: Rachel Rosales
Typesetting: Zach Parker
Author photo: Jeff Meyers

ISBN: 978-1-7335356-7-0

TABLE OF CONTENTS

PREFACE

SOLOMON AS DRIVER'S ED TEACHER

The ability to drive a car is a necessary skill for most people in industrialized countries. As a result, it has become a rite of passage into adulthood.

At the time I'm writing this, I've taught three children how to drive, and each one of them experienced not only changing abilities but expanded working knowledge. Shortly before they started driving, they showed little awareness of the network of roads and locations around our home, even when traveling on familiar routes to familiar places. I would ask them what direction we were heading or where I should turn and they usually had no idea. They were just along for the ride. Since they relied on someone else to drive, they didn't waste mental capacity on such things. (It was somewhat flattering. They trusted me to steer them where they needed to go.)

But when they got behind the steering wheel, that changed quickly. Suddenly, the maps inside their heads expanded to include virtually the entire metro area and surrounding counties. Learning to drive gave them a new dominion. They grew in their knowledge to accommodate their new powers for a larger realm. It was a profound transformation. When they took on adult responsibilities, they transitioned to adult thinking.

So let's think how a child develops when he learns how to drive.

When a parent sits in the passenger seat next to a son or daughter, that parent will typically rehearse a few principles:

- The pedal on the left slows and stops the car when pressed.
- The pedal on the right increases engine power and thus speed.
- You only use your right foot on the pedals.
- You turn the steering wheel the way you want the car to turn.

When the new driver tries to apply these and other instructions for the first time, the results are not pretty. The instructions are true and the new "driver" may remember them all accurately, but his attempts to follow the instructions are a jerky, frightening mess. The problem is the *youth has new immense power available to him*, far more than he's used to. Going forward happens with more speed and stopping happens more abruptly.

But if you find a relatively safe place and practice small things, progressing from one level of difficulty to another, you eventually become a driver.

Does that mean the driver remembers the rules of operating an automobile more accurately than he did before?

Mostly not. It means that, *when he gets into a car, it becomes part of his body*. He no more needs to remember which pedal to push at which moment than he needs to remember how to swing his arms to balance as he walks. He "just does it." Maybe there's a brief adjustment when he has to drive an unfamiliar vehicle, but in general he controls the vehicle with almost as little thought as it takes him to control his legs and feet when he needs to walk somewhere.

Thinking about how the steering wheel works while driving would be like going into a flower shop to pick out roses by first imagining a red patch and finding a flower that matched it. It would be like thinking about where each foot needs to go to move from the couch in the living room to the kitchen sink. Functional human beings don't operate that way.

Of course, a car doesn't become a biological entity that attaches to you, but through the controls and the neurological adaptations your body is trained to make to those controls, it becomes an extension of yourself. *You* turn left or right or stop or speed up. You don't think about making *the car* do those things unless something goes wrong and it doesn't respond as you expect.

As a result of the process of guided practice, you develop new abilities that in turn require and elicit new mental capacities. Suddenly, you become more aware of where you live and how that relates to places you need to travel to.

◊

So what does this have to do with Proverbs? Is Solomon a driver's ed teacher?

The process of becoming a driver is similar to the process of growing from an infant to an older child. A baby has little control over his extremities. He actually becomes curious about them as if they are alien things. Thus babies put their hands into their mouths. But as they grow, they bring their hands and feet under their dominion. They gain control over their limbs, learning new skills.

Think of a baby's first attempts to crawl or walk. These movements are hesitant and exploratory, not unlike someone trying to drive for the first time. But invariably, learning the skill of crawling and then of walking means they stop having to consciously control their hands and feet. The first faltering steps involved in learning to walk give way to running. The child no longer needs to think about placing one foot in front of the other. Worrying about that would slow him down or even trip him up. The child is able to "drive" his own body.

And if a toddler's growth is like learning to drive a car, so is the growth spurt that marks the transition to full adulthood like learning to drive. Young men and women sometimes change so rapidly they feel like aliens in their own skins. Voices change, muscles grow, and they become aware of new desires.

It is not uncommon for a young man to become somewhat clumsier for a time until he learns to pilot himself better.

But this second stage of development is different from what happened earlier. A child grows from infancy to toddlerhood with only the beginnings of moral awareness dictated to him by his parents. A teen learning to drive has to consider ethics, too. A young child who runs when he should walk isn't risking as much as a driver who hates being restrained by the speed limit. Controlling one's impulses takes on new importance because of the potential consequences. Paying attention to where one is and who is around you is much more important for a driver than for a child walking. Bad habits of hurrying, not paying attention, or trying to get ahead of others, involve more dangerous risks for a driver. Similarly, the bad habits, attitudes, and vices of a young adult can have more severe consequences than those of a young child.

But with these more severe consequences comes a new way to address the problems: You can talk to a young adult going through this process. Just as learning to drive is an opportunity to break bad habits and learn better ones, becoming an adult gives you a chance to leave childish ways behind and get better at piloting yourself through life.

That's what Solomon is doing in Proverbs. He's using words to help a young man drive the mysterious highway of indeterminate distance and unknown road conditions that is his future. He wants to help you master yourself to navigate to your final destination.

Proverbs is direction for making wisdom a part of your body.

INTRODUCTION

This is not a commentary on Proverbs.

This book is an introduction to Proverbs as a guide to life. Of course, this book does not exhaust all the riches of Proverbs and, as a guide to life, Proverbs is read correctly only in the context of the whole Bible. That's why I often appeal to other Scripture, from Genesis to the general epistles.

So let's consider what I think is the basic purpose of Proverbs.

Proverbs is written to young men (and everyone else) to encourage and instruct them to become kings and not to remain slaves.

Let's unpack this claim.

Perhaps you find it odd that the statement doesn't mention becoming a *Christian* king. From the perspective of Proverbs, there is no way to become and remain a stable ruler without God's favor. The instructions in Proverbs presuppose that God governs our lives and that, while he often honors people who follow his wisdom to whatever extent, he is not obligated to bless them if they do not recognize his love, authority, and trustworthiness. Ultimately, to say that Proverbs is written to young men to instruct them to become *Christian* kings would imply that there is a secular version available. Obviously, pagan or secular rulers have often reigned and continued to do so, but Proverbs sees them as holding a place that could soon be taken away from them. According to Proverbs, the only wise way to become a king is to acknowledge God as the high king.

Proverbs is mostly written by Solomon, with contributions made by Hezekiah and King Lemuel (from his royal mother: 31:1). There are a couple of contributors who *might* not be royalty—"the wise" (24:23) and Agur (30:1)—but the book mostly comes from kings. In the large section that comes from King Solomon, he addresses the listener or reader as "my son." One might think, then, that Proverbs is intended only for princes, who are heirs to the throne. Thus, in 8:15-16, Wisdom says

> By me kings reign,
> and rulers decree what is just;
> by me princes rule,
> and nobles, all who govern justly.

But the intended audience of Proverbs is more than just those who are set to inherit political authority. Proverbs was published as wisdom for everyone. In some important sense, we are all supposed to become kings in this life and the next. We all need to pursue wisdom because we all need to be able to rule well. The story of Solomon's request for wisdom to equip him to rule (1 Kgs. 3:5-14) is a story for all of us.

In one sense, Proverbs seems to be Wisdom's call to everyone to seek to be true sons (and also daughters) of Solomon.

A king is someone who has authority over a kingdom. Proverbs, as we will see, teaches that we all ordinarily come to possess an area of the world over which we have authority. Each of us needs wisdom in order to deal with our kingdom—whatever area God gives us authority over.

Young men are in a transitional stage. They are on the cusp of adulthood. Proverbs is especially aimed at them, though everyone can and should profit from the book.

◊

Why did I write that Proverbs teaches us (especially young men) to not *remain* slaves?

Because, children start off in life as virtual slaves.

"Man is born free and everywhere he is in chains," wrote Jean-Jacques Rousseau.[1] Solomon and the Apostle Paul would tell you that man is born a slave as a baby that is destined to become a ruler, the only kind of free person that there is. There is nothing wrong with a child being a slave, but it is shameful if he remains a slave when he is supposed to mature into freedom. The impulse to maintain childhood is foolishness and leads to more foolishness.

As Paul wrote:

> I mean that the heir, as long as he is a child, is no different from a slave, though he is the owner of everything, but he is under guardians and managers until the date set by his father (Gal. 4:1–2).

A child is a slave because others give him orders. If a child's parents hire a tutor to teach him, that tutor will be a mere employee of the parents. He won't be a member of the family. But the child will be required to submit to his authority. The child, while he is being taught, is required to heed a mere hired hand.

As a child outgrows the "slavery" of childhood, another change is supposed to occur. As a child becomes a man, his judgment is supposed to improve. According to Paul, Christ gave pastors and other gifts to the Church...

> ...until we all attain to the unity of the faith and of the knowledge of the Son of God, to mature manhood, to the measure of the stature of the fullness of Christ, so that we may no longer be children, tossed to and fro by the waves and carried about by every wind of doctrine, by human cunning, by craftiness in deceitful schemes (Eph. 4:13–14).

We learn from this analogy that children are like slaves not only in how they are treated in the family social hierarchy, but also in their lack of discernment. They are vulnerable to those who would exploit them by deceit. Their emotions and desires can be used to manipulate them. They are easily enslaved. A mature adult should not be so vulnerable.

So a child is a slave and there's nothing wrong with that. He has been given parents to protect him and allow him to grow up to become a mature adult who has discernment.

But what can go wrong?

A young child often sees adults as possessing an amazing amount of freedom. They get to go to bed when they want. They drink alcoholic beverages if they want to do so. They decide when to eat ice cream and how much. They determine their own limits in watching video entertainment. No one tells them (a child thinks) what to do.

Thus, a child's impression of adult freedom is something like being a child without parental supervision. Freedom is seen as getting to play whenever one wants. As a child grows up, he should understand that this is not a proper conception of adulthood, but sinful human beings are prone to wishful thinking even when they are smart enough to know better. They resist the Apostle Paul's wisdom: "When I was a child, I spoke like a child, I thought like a child, I reasoned like a child. When I became a man, I gave up childish ways" (1 Cor. 13:11).

When you refuse to give up childish ways, you don't thereby really remain a child. A young man has more intelligence, knowledge, and strength than he did as a child. Sexual development is also a new element in his life. Yet, if he doesn't embrace wisdom, he will be prone to treat these new interests and abilities as if they were new toys, rather than as adult gifts and adult responsibilities. And if this continues, he will be ruled by these now out-of-control desires and destructive habits. He will act like a slave rather than a king. Proverbs warns that he will truly become a slave if he refuses to depart from such foolishness.

Science fiction author Frank Herbert once wrote, "Seek freedom and become captive of your desires. Seek discipline and find your liberty."[2] Likewise, Solomon is concerned that his sons will be taken captive by an adulteress: "Do not desire her beauty in your heart, and do not let her capture you with her eyelashes" (Prov. 6:25). He explains, "The righteousness of the upright delivers them, but the treacherous are taken captive by their lust" (Prov. 11:6).

If you're a captive, then you're not much of a king.

THE STRUCTURE OF PROVERBS

Proverbs has seven sections:

1. *Proverbs 1–9*: "The proverbs of Solomon, son of David, king of Israel..." This first section is much more obviously structured around major themes, such as wisdom and foolishness and sex and violence.

2. *Proverbs 10—22:16*: "The proverbs of Solomon..." Here we get a huge collection of sayings in an order that is harder to understand.

3. *Proverbs 22:17—24:22*: "Incline your ear, and hear the words of the wise..." The context makes clear that these "words of the wise" are a separate collection of sayings.

4. *Proverbs 24:23–34*: "These also are sayings of the wise..."

5. *Proverbs 25–29*: "These also are proverbs of Solomon which the men of Hezekiah king of Judah copied..."

6. *Proverbs 30*: "The words of Agur son of Jakeh. The oracle..."

7. *Proverbs 31*: "The words of King Lemuel. An oracle that his mother taught him..."

Much of Proverbs seems to be made up of aphorisms (especially in chapters 10–29). There is probably more going on here, since one does not normally use the same aphorisms over again in a collection. But Proverbs often repeats material verbatim in close proximity. For example:

- "righteousness delivers from death" (10:2; 11:4)
- "humility comes before honor" (15:33; 18:12)
- "There is a way that seems right to a man, but its end is the way to death" (14:12; 16:25)

It would be difficult to preach through Proverbs because at times you would be preaching the same sermon more than once.

This indicates that Proverbs is not necessarily meant to be preached through. It doesn't follow a simple narrative or argument, but it does have a design rather than being a random collection of sayings. We often need to hear the same things over and over again, whether restated in different words or repeated verbatim. Proverbs is probably meant to be read repeatedly or memorized. It is offered as a tool for people to constantly recite to themselves or to one another to remind them of how God wants them to deal with other people and the world.

The purpose of Proverbs is stated at the outset:

> To know wisdom and instruction,
> to understand words of insight,
> to receive instruction in wise dealing,
> in righteousness, justice, and equity;
> to give prudence to the simple,
> knowledge and discretion to the youth—
> Let the wise hear and increase in learning,
> and the one who understands obtain guidance,
> to understand a proverb and a saying,
> the words of the wise and their riddles (1:2–6).

This is somewhat odd. If the purpose of the book is "to understand a proverb," why give us a collection of proverbs? Where's the explanation of how to understand a proverb? Where's the solution to the riddles?

It seems that Proverbs is a path beckoning you to understanding. It is a riddle that you must wrestle with. God is treating you, again, as a king: "It is the glory of God to conceal things, but the glory of kings is to search things out" (25:2).

Proverbs shows you how to understand its sayings and riddles simply by repeatedly exposing you to them, even exposing you sometimes to the same ones in a different context.

These are some of the reasons why I did not attempt to write a commentary on Proverbs. Instead, this book is a reader's guide to Proverbs that lays out some important themes in Proverbs. The goal is to get you reading and memorizing Proverbs as you seek and find wisdom for your life.

I describe Proverbs in this book as containing nine lessons. There are other lessons in the book, but these nine are important and are good to keep in mind whenever you read the book.

Chapter 1 argues more comprehensively that the main theme in Proverbs is becoming, by habit and attitude, a person who is better able to accomplish what God has called him to do as an adult. Proverbs assumes that one was taught God's basic commandments as a child. But the challenge is to develop habits and attitudes that make living according to those commandments easier.

Chapter 2 discusses the two major temptations described in the first section of Proverbs (chs. 1–9) as they relate to God's blueprint for humanity (Gen. 1:29). The two great sins that Solomon warns against are robbery and adultery. Growing up to despise honest work and despise marriage is self-destructive, thwarting who we were created to be. (Despising marriage is not the same as remaining single. Not every man or woman is called to get married.)

Chapters 3 and 4 elaborate more on what attitudes and habits Proverbs recommends (and warns against) for work and productivity. Chapter 5 considers the warnings against adultery and related issues.

The next two chapters discuss speech and the habits and attitudes that will make one's words a means of empowerment rather than self-sabotage. Chapter 6 covers a couple of broad principles of using and not using one's voice, while Chapter 7 dives into some details regarding judicious talking and listening.

Since Proverbs says a lot about success and not causing one's own failure, I felt it was necessary to spend Chapter 8 explaining the limits of wisdom for the outcomes of your life. Solomon recommends wisdom, but it is not a magical means to make all your dreams come true.

Finally, Chapter 9 emphasizes the lessons of the book by showing how the Bible presents godliness as something that can and should involve training; learning godliness is much like learning a sport or how to play a musical instrument. The chapter ends by pointing out that, while wisdom should be embraced at all ages, the younger you start, the better off you will be.

◊

How important is Proverbs? While the book can be applied to everyone, it is especially addressed to a son at the edge of maturity. As such, Proverbs is distinctly concerned with what it means to be a man—a man as opposed to a child and, to some extent, a man as opposed to a woman. (I say, to some extent, because women are supposed to benefit from the book as well.) It is the Bible's recipe for masculinity and has correctives to many natural temptations to false views of life that attract young males.

1

You Must Rule Yourself

All that is gold does not glitter,
Not all those who wander are lost;
The old that is strong does not wither,
Deep roots are not reached by the frost.
From the ashes a fire shall be woken,
A light from the shadows shall spring;
Renewed shall be blade that was broken,
The crownless again shall be king.
     — J. R. R. Tolkien, *The Fellowship of the Ring*[3]

By me kings reign,
     and rulers decree what is just;
by me princes rule,
     and nobles, all who govern justly.
     — Wisdom (Prov. 8:15–16)

How can Proverbs assert that wisdom enables kings to rule and yet recommend wisdom for everyone? If Proverbs envisions a world with rulers, then you would think that there would have to be a larger class of people who are ruled. So how can everyone be called upon to rule? Do not masters imply slaves?

These questions were addressed in the introduction, but I want to elaborate on the answer and show you how it is found in Proverbs.

To understand Solomon's reasoning consider a fictional story about a man and his slave:

David thought the interview had gone well so far. Huxley Industries needed a slave to answer phones, keep records, and do other office work. David needed some better income, and he had a slave to rent. His slave could easily do the jobs that they needed to be done.

"So, can your slave be here by 7:30 every weekday morning?"

David's heart lurched. "You start that early?"

"Well, we need him ready to go before others come to work. We found this position works better if he starts a half hour earlier."

"Oh."

"Is that a problem?" Sharon the interviewer sounded completely nonjudgmental about David's slave. He was thankful for her professionalism.

"Well, I have my slave during most of the day," said David, hating he had to admit the truth out loud. "Body is a good slave and I'm sure he could do the work here."

"But...?"

"But I'm not completely his sole owner. His other master may make that 7:30 start time difficult to meet."

"Someone else has ownership that early in the morning?"

David shook his head. "Not in the morning, but usually late at night. Wine, Women, and Song are part owners from about 9 p.m. until pretty late. Getting up that early might be a problem."

Sharon nodded. "That was actually why this position didn't work with the last slave we tried to rent from someone."

"Did Wine, Women, and Song have part ownership?"

"No," said Sharon, "I think it was Late Night Television. It kept the slave up at night and when the other owner got full control back in the morning, the slave was too groggy to work for us effectively."

David sighed.

"I appreciate talking to you about the job," said Sharon. "But you have to understand that lots of slaves can do the tasks we need done. Our problem isn't the tasks themselves but the simple fact that many owners are not really total owners. You can't really rent out a slave if you already share him with other masters."

Rule or Be Ruled

Hopefully, the meaning of that little story is obvious. The position of David and his slave, aptly named "Body," is that of any person who wants the rewards of being a valued employee but doesn't seem to have intentional control over some of his actions. He is subject to what might be called "compulsive behavior" that undermines his goals in life.

You know what you need to do and should do, and in some sense, you "want" to do it. But your various urges and short-term desires sabotage your plans because you don't rule yourself. Compulsive behavior or bad habits overwhelm your plans to reach your goals or to develop into the kind of person who can have goals.

While we in the modern world tend to juxtapose freedom and slavery, Proverbs more often contrasts authority with slavery. Solomon believes that wisdom involves managing what authority you have and gaining more while folly leads to slavery. Thus, "the fool will be servant to the wise of heart" (11:29b).

There is a common conception or model of biblical wisdom that portrays it as something you use while seated and thinking. Solomon was a wise king and he certainly did just that. So we get Proverbs like "The one who states his case first seems right, until the other comes and examines him" (18:17).

But many matters addressed in Proverbs seem pretty far from an official courtroom situation. For example: "Say to wisdom, 'You are my sister,' and call insight your intimate friend, to keep you from the forbidden woman, from the adulteress with her smooth words" (7:4–5). Wisdom in this case is associated with the character required to stay away from sex outside of marriage.

This explains why Proverbs is mostly about character development and avoiding bad habits. Fools become slaves to others because they allow themselves to become slaves to emotions, behaviors, and false stories that justify them. I already mentioned this in the introduction, but Proverbs reiterates the point in several ways:

- "Whoever is slow to anger is better than the mighty, and he who *rules his spirit* than he who takes a city" (16:32).

- "A man without self-control is like a city broken into and left without walls" (25:28).

- "The righteousness of the upright delivers them, but the treacherous are *taken captive by their lust*" (11:6).

- "Do not desire her beauty in your heart, and do not let her *capture* you with her eyelashes" (6:25).

- "The *desire* of the sluggard *kills him*, for his *hands refuse* to labor" (21:25).

- "Do not *give your strength to women*, your ways to those who destroy kings" (31:3).

- "Wine is a mocker, strong drink a brawler, and whoever is led astray by it is not wise" (20:1).

- "*The iniquities of the wicked ensnare him*, and he is *held fast in the cords* of his sin. He dies for lack of discipline, and because of his great folly he is led astray" (5:22–23).

If you don't govern yourself, you will be governed by others, and your own impulses will be the reins they use to lead you. Or, if we think of this in the context of growing up: When you leave your parents behind, you must learn to parent yourself. If you don't become your own effective parent, Solomon warns, you'll end up being ruled by other "parents" who probably don't care about your best interests. For example, "The hand of the diligent will rule, while the slothful will be put to forced labor" (12:24). Contrast that warning with the commendation of the ants who work "without having any chief, officer, or ruler" to tell them what to do (Prov. 6:7). Ants seem to take care of themselves. We should do so, too.

Here's another way of looking at the issue of governing one's own body and actions, using speech as an example:

- "When words are many, transgression is not lacking, but whoever restrains his lips is prudent" (10:19).

- "Whoever restrains his words has knowledge, and he who has a cool spirit is a man of understanding" (17:27).

- "Whoever keeps his mouth and his tongue keeps himself out of trouble" (21:23).

We will discuss speech some more in a later section, but notice that in the first two verses it is assumed that words are plentiful. They are so plentiful that you don't want to indiscriminately release them. You have to select the right ones. Likewise, you have to keep (or guard) your speech because of what will otherwise come out of your mouth.

Thinking involves making connections and your brain, at some level, often produces much that isn't appropriate, helpful, or productive. So a job you have to master as you grow up is choosing which words to share. You have to get in the habit of *not* sharing all the words you could.

Otherwise, bad things can happen. "A fool's lips walk into a fight, and his mouth invites a beating" (Prov. 18:6). The ethical problem is that people assume all their words are important and must be expressed. That need to express whatever you think is a kind of selfishness, and it is often also a form of self-destructive behavior.

If you want to be a ruler, you need to master your desires, your body, your self. A son grows up to be a king by ruling over himself.

Taking Dominion

James writes that not many should be teachers. Why?

> For we all stumble in many ways. And if anyone does not stumble in what he says, he is a perfect man, able also to bridle his whole body. If we put bits into the mouths of horses so that they obey us, we guide their whole bodies as well....
>
> For every kind of beast and bird, of reptile and sea creature, can be tamed and has been tamed by mankind, but no human being can tame the tongue....
>
> Who is wise and understanding among you? By his good conduct let him show his works in the meekness of wisdom. But if you have bitter jealousy and selfish ambition in your hearts, do not boast and be false to the truth. This is not the wisdom that comes down from above, but is earthly, unspiritual, demonic. For where jealousy and selfish ambition exist, there will be disorder and every vile practice. But the wisdom from above is first pure, then peaceable, gentle, open to reason, full of mercy and good fruits, impartial and sincere. And a harvest of righteousness is sown in peace by those who make peace (Jas. 3:2-18).

That isn't all of James 3 but it hits some points that are highly relevant to Proverbs and probably are meant to refer to Proverbs. James' description of true Wisdom reminds us of Proverbs. So notice that James compares taking dominion over one's tongue to taking dominion over animals.

That concept goes back to the foundation of humanity's creation. We read in Genesis 1:26–28 that the basic charge to humanity from the beginning was to take dominion over creation, including all the animals. James points to humanity's fulfillment of the mandate to take dominion over the earth as related to control over one's speech. If humans are called to subdue the animals, much more should they gain control over their mouths. And if they're called to take dominion over their mouths, then they are likewise called to take dominion over their hands and feet.

This points to the fact that every descendant of Adam and Eve is called to rule over a portion of creation *including himself* — perhaps even *especially* himself. The call to Adam and Eve is a call to all of us to be kings and queens, subduing an appropriate territory to God's glory. This territory may not be much, but God's promise is that, if we are faithful in small things, we will be given responsibility over great things.

Genesis 1:26–28 is commonly called the Dominion Mandate. There are many who think Jesus gave a new form of the Dominion Mandate after his resurrection, as recorded at the end of Matthew's Gospel.

> Now the eleven disciples went to Galilee, to the mountain to which Jesus had directed them. And when they saw him they worshiped him, but some doubted. And Jesus came and said to them, "All authority in heaven and on earth has been given to me. Go therefore and make disciples of all nations, baptizing them in the name of the Father and of the Son and of the Holy Spirit, teaching them to observe all that I have commanded you. And behold, I am with you always, to the end of the age" (Matt. 28:16–20).

This passage, commonly known as the Great Commission, is often reduced to evangelism and maybe Christian education and activism. But think about what is included: "teaching them to observe all that I have commanded you." Obviously, any time a person teaches another how to bring his life into closer conformity to God's word, he is participating in the Great Commission.

But what if the teacher and the student are the same person? If a Christian reads the Bible and changes his behavior to conform to what he reads, how is that any less a fulfillment of part of the Great Commission? Is the person not teaching himself better to observe Jesus' commands?

And teaching involves more than relaying information. As we will see in more detail in Chapter 9, teaching often includes *training* (1 Tim. 4:7, 8). For you as a Christian, following Jesus' commands includes diligent practice in obedience to God, becoming the kind of person who is more prone to obey God and less prone to disobey him.

James spoke of the tongue as a creature that you need to bring under control as part of the Dominion Mandate. And the Great Commission not only calls you to disciple the nations, but to disciple your hands and feet. Remember how Solomon describes unruly body parts:

> There are six things that the LORD hates,
>   seven that are an abomination to him:
> haughty eyes, a lying tongue,
>   and hands that shed innocent blood,
> a heart that devises wicked plans,
>   feet that make haste to run to evil,
> a false witness who breathes out lies,
>   and one who sows discord among brothers (Prov. 6:16-19).

The point here is not that evil "dwells" in any specific limb or organ, but that the ways sin leads us to habitually act—how we get accustomed to using our eyes, tongues, hands, hearts, and feet—are hostile to God. The Great Commission, in a sense, calls you to "go" to your limbs and train them in new habits. Thus:

Let not sin therefore reign in your mortal body, to make you obey its passions. Do not present your members to sin as instruments for unrighteousness, but present yourselves to God as those who have been brought from death to life, and your members to God as instruments for righteousness (Rom. 6:12–13).

What It Takes to Get Married

Perhaps my illustration of the man who needed to rent out a slave is too weird. But consider a real-life example that happens all the time: a marriage.

When a man and a woman get married, they promise themselves to each other. The bridegroom offers his self to the bride and vice versa. The assumption is that they are each in a position to actually give what they promise.

But how often is that completely true? While the average bride and groom in a wedding are legally free to marry the other, how much real freedom do they possess to truly offer and give themselves to the other?

To a *certain* extent, of course, you can't learn how to give yourself in marriage until you get married to a particular woman. You are promising to learn how you need to change to become the perfect husband (not perfect in a generic way but perfect to your specific wife) and then to do so. That can't be figured out *completely* before marriage. You have to learn and grow and adapt.

But there are ways, as you develop and grow as an individual Christian man, that you can make yourself more or less suitable to be a husband in general. To put it another way, your promise at the ceremony to be a husband will probably be better executed if you work beforehand on being the kind of person who can keep such a promise. When you officially give yourself to a woman in marriage, you need to be free of habits and vices that would hamper your ability to offer yourself to your bride as a beneficial husband.

9

Paradoxically, such freedom comes from the discipline of slavery. Slavery to oneself.

I mean "slavery to oneself" as an integrated decision-maker with a mission as a human being in God's world, rather than slavery to the bits of you, whether immature or downright sinful, that you can't understand. You want to be the servant of your goals as a Christian man rather than the slave of impulses that prompt you to act in ways that are detrimental to those goals.

If you can't master yourself, you have no capacity to offer yourself to another in any significant way. Sometimes, two people take vows to each other who have invisible "spouses" already chained to their hands, feet, eyes, and mouths. They are slaves to ambitions, greed, vices, assorted addictions, and fears.

Marriage has to force real change on a person in order to work. The person has to realize that the vow to belong to another entails a vow to capture and dominate one's self so that one has a person to offer to the other. That's why my absolutist language should not be taken too literally. You can indeed offer yourself to your spouse, but it probably involves a promise to capture more of yourself and bring those parts into the family.

BECOME THE MAN YOUR FUTURE SELF WOULD BE GRATEFUL FOR

Why am I talking about a person as if he were a collection of opposing forces?

Because that is the way we are. Sin aggravates the problem, but anyone who sees a baby discovering its own hands and feet should realize that the process of maturation is a process of integrating parts into a whole, unified person. Remember Paul's description of childhood as "tossed to and fro by the waves and carried about by every wind" (Eph. 4:14).

God created people with multiple desires, abilities, and possible goals depending on their circumstances. We needed to be created this way because there were many different tasks God wanted future members of the human race to complete. So we will all have many different desires that we have to choose from.

A person who wants money does not also want to be arrested and get a criminal record, but if he lets his desire for money spur the wrong kind of action, he will get that outcome. Another wants money too, but also wants to please God and have a sense of accomplishment by earning it. That stark choice shows an obvious difference between wisdom and foolishness, but other choices also involve that difference though it may not be as obvious.

If you saw a parent allowing his young child to eat whatever he wanted, buying him candy whenever he asked, you would suspect the parent was being negligent, permitting the child to fulfill desires that would lead to his own unhappiness, though the child may be totally unaware of what's at stake. A good parent makes a child abstain from many of his desires in order to preserve a future for him in which he can be healthy and happy. A parent's limits on a child are not designed to make him unhappy but to empower him as a human being.

So when you "parent" yourself according to God's guidance, his rules and counsel are not designed to limit you but to empower you. Wisdom involves the power to discipline yourself in that direction, and in many cases to see how God's ways are the ways of life and all alternatives lead to death. As Solomon says, "Desire without knowledge is not good" (Prov. 19:2). You can enjoy good things—like sleep (3:24)—but you must limit that enjoyment to avoid something bad—like poverty (20:13). Thus: "Whoever gets sense loves his own soul; he who keeps understanding will discover good" (19:8). Compare that with the warning from Wisdom earlier: "but he who fails to find me injures himself; all who hate me love death" (8:36).

Very few people think they love "death"—whether literal death or a dead end situation. But most children eating too much candy don't love tooth decay. The point is that being an adult means weighing options and deciding what's compatible between immediate desires, short-term objectives, and long-term goals. It means developing habits and attitudes that allow for this freedom rather than vices that chain you and frustrate your efforts. It involves telling yourself stories that encourage wisdom rather than lies that promote folly.

A person who thinks that God's advice about loving sleep too much is oppressive might try to defy his wisdom. If he does so, he probably won't keep the freedom to sleep very long. "The hand of the diligent will rule, while the slothful will be put to forced labor" (Prov. 12:24). By limiting sleep *on his own*, a wise son will gain *more* freedom to afford sleep and many other things, just as a child raised to avoid dental problems might find more enjoyment (of candy and many other things) in the long run.

Wisdom is for our empowerment and enjoyment in life, not to oppress us.

God as king doesn't want to rule slaves, but he wants a company of deputy rulers whom he entrusts with powers and responsibilities. By seeking and gaining wisdom, we grow in our understanding of how to take dominion, discovering in many cases how God's commandments make sense and why disobedience is senseless.

And who does God elevate for higher responsibilities? Those who treated their smaller responsibilities not as meaningless chores but as opportunities to be diligent and faithful and to grow in wisdom. Remember the words from Jesus' parable of the stewards in Matthew 25: "You have been faithful over a little; I will set you over much" (v. 21).

Your Life is Your Kingdom

So as you rule yourself you also have to manage the particular responsibilities and opportunities that God gives you. Solomon (as we know from King Hezekiah's scribes) viewed anyone's job as a kind of kingdom:

> Know well the condition of your flocks,
>   and give attention to your herds,
> for riches do not last forever;
>   and does a crown endure to all generations?
> When the grass is gone and the new growth appears
>   and the vegetation of the mountains is gathered,
> the lambs will provide your clothing,
>   and the goats the price of a field.
> There will be enough goats' milk for your food,
>   for the food of your household
>   and maintenance for your girls (Prov. 27:23–27).

Is this an exhortation to kings to stay alert, using being a shepherd as a metaphor, or is it an exhortation to a shepherd to regard his responsibility as his personal kingdom? The metaphor works both ways. Solomon knew from the story of his father that being faithful as a shepherd trained him to be a warrior in battle and then a king.

> And David said to Saul, "Let no man's heart fail because of him [Goliath]. Your servant will go and fight with this Philistine."
> And Saul said to David, "You are not able to go against this Philistine to fight with him, for you are but a youth, and he has been a man of war from his youth."
> But David said to Saul, "Your servant used to keep sheep for his father. And when there came a lion, or a bear, and took a lamb from the flock, I went after him and struck him and delivered it out of his mouth. And if he arose against me, I caught him by his beard and struck him and killed him. Your servant has struck

down both lions and bears, and this uncircumcised Philistine shall be like one of them, for he has defied the armies of the living God."

And David said, "The LORD who delivered me from the paw of the lion and from the paw of the bear will deliver me from the hand of this Philistine."

And Saul said to David, "Go, and the LORD be with you!" (1 Sam. 17:32–37).

Throughout history, many sons commanded to do jobs for their parents have felt like slaves, not kings. Solomon offers a different perspective. He suggests that these smaller areas of responsibility are kingdoms. If you want to be a wise king of a larger domain, you need to learn to rule over what you have.

God has placed you in circumstances wherein you can gain mastery over yourself as you master your responsibilities. These circumstances may not be what you want, but they are not a prison. They are a launching pad, *if* you will use them to learn how to rule.

PULLING THE SWORD FROM THE STONE

Since Proverbs is about kings, let's consider the story of King Arthur drawing Excalibur. I don't know if there is any understandable origin to the myth of a man being designated king by being the only person who can pull a sword from a stone, but it is suggestive as a metaphor for developing character. A sword trapped in a stone is no good to anyone. It is useless. Someone has to pull it out in order to make it useful.

Likewise, you have more potential than you realize. If you didn't, Proverbs would not spend so much time warning you of ways you can weaken yourself and obstruct yourself from achieving good. Such advice acknowledges that you can and will accomplish great things if only you will take ownership of yourself. Your proven character is your greatest potential asset, your primary weapon in the war of life.

What Charles Spurgeon said to his students wishing to become pastors actually applies to all Christians in all occupations:

> Every workman knows the necessity of keeping his tools in a good state of repair, for "if the iron be blunt, and he do not whet the edge, then must he put to more strength." If the workman lose the edge from his adze, he knows that there will be a greater draught upon his energies, or his work will be badly done....
>
> We are, in a certain sense, our own tools, and therefore must keep ourselves in order. If I want to preach the gospel, I can only use my own voice; therefore I must train my vocal powers. I can only think with my own brains, and feel with my own heart, and therefore I must educate my intellectual and emotional faculties. I can only weep and agonize for souls in my own renewed nature, therefore must I watchfully maintain the tenderness which was in Christ Jesus. It will be in vain for me to stock my library, or organize societies, or project schemes, if I neglect the culture of myself; for books, and agencies, and systems, are only remotely the instruments of my holy calling; my own spirit, soul, and body, are my nearest machinery for sacred service; my spiritual faculties, and my inner life, are my battle axe and weapons of war.[4]

Whether sword or battle axe is your preferred image, the point is that the most important tool you can have to deal with the world is your own self. It is a tool that can be neglected and grow less useful. Or you can sharpen it and protect its edge.

Solomon wants you to pull your sword free and be a king.

2

THE GENESIS OF ADULTHOOD

There are two methods, or means, and only two, whereby man's needs and desires can be satisfied. One is the production and exchange of wealth; this is the economic means. The other is the uncompensated appropriation of wealth produced by others; this is the political means.

- Albert Jay Nock[5]

The term "tree of life" occurs in only three books in the Bible: Genesis, Revelation, and Proverbs. It is easy to understand why it would be mentioned in two of those. Genesis records how humanity lost the Tree of Life, and Revelation tells us that it has been restored to us.

But why is it in Proverbs?

One might be tempted to think it is just a handy metaphor, but the first mention of the Tree introduces Wisdom's role in the creation story.

[Wisdom] is a tree of life to those who lay hold of her;
　　those who hold her fast are called blessed.
The LORD by wisdom founded the earth;
　　by understanding he established the heavens;
by his knowledge the deeps broke open,
　　and the clouds drop down the dew (Prov. 3:18–20).

Later in the first book of Proverbs (1–9), Solomon portrays wisdom personified and she exults in how she was present when God created the world (8:22–31).

In the last chapter, I mentioned the Dominion Mandate as a way of understanding how humans are expected to grow as rulers over themselves and over their areas of responsibility. That's not just a handy analogy. Solomon spends time assuring us that the creation story is vital to wisdom, and thus it is a key to understanding Proverbs.

In fact, Proverbs is a much more understandable book if we are familiar with Genesis. Besides the tree of life and creation,

- There is a lot about sons being a source of sorrow to their mothers, who had originally praised God they had gotten a man with the help of Yahweh.

- Fools refuse to listen to rebukes or instruction, when a wise person says, "If you do well, will you not be accepted?"

- There are warnings about the sons of God desiring the daughters of men.

- Violence receives a lot of attention.

- What kind of counsel a wife and mother gives is discussed.

- They both address what sort of woman ought to be valued as marriage material.

- Wives are shown to be a gift from God rather than a human discovery.

- Diligence is promised to be rewarded with dominion.

- Though wisdom is more valuable than the gold of Havilah, it is a way to get that too, if God gives the opportunity.

- There are springs of life.

- And how cities are built is an important issue.

It is easy to read Proverbs as a meditation on Genesis. Indeed the stories in Genesis may explain why Christians often have a hard time with Proverbs. The book of Proverbs is difficult for many reasons, one of which is how far "theology" has drifted from the story of the Bible. I'm not necessarily talking about false theology. Even correct theology, as it is often communicated, turns Proverbs into alien territory.

Maybe I can explain what the problem is this way:

If you are a *believer* in a religion that is best expressed as four spiritual laws or a flow-chart or a chart about the dispensations of history or a scheme of double predestination or many other things (some of which may be true; the issue is not veracity but primacy), then it will be a mystery to you why God wrote the book of Proverbs and put it in our Bibles.

But if you are a *practitioner* of a religion centered on a story that begins with how God made men and women to relate to him and one another as they take dominion over the world, and move downstream from their garden home, and find gold, and start trading, and have to raise children and eventually build cities that are supposed to further reflect the glory of God, then it will make intuitive sense why the book of Proverbs had to be included as Scripture.

So what kind of practice is Solomon advocating in Proverbs?

Stepping into the Office of Adam

Proverbs makes a big deal out of relating wisdom to creation and exhorting young men to find and gain wisdom. Genesis presents Adam and Eve as created adults. When they had their first child, they encountered something new and strange: a human being who could not walk or talk and who was small and frail. Babies are as human as their parents, but they are not capable of the tasks that adults have to perform.

This means that, when a young man is at the threshold of adulthood, he is about to fully assume his role as another "Adam" on the world stage. He's in a position to pursue the mandate to take dominion and perhaps even to multiply.

> And God blessed them. And God said to them, "Be fruitful and multiply and fill the earth and subdue it, and have dominion over the fish of the sea and over the birds of the heavens and over every living thing that moves on the earth." And God said, "Behold, I have given you every plant yielding seed that is on the face of all the earth, and every tree with seed in its fruit. You shall have them for food. And to every beast of the earth and to every bird of the heavens and to everything that creeps on the earth, everything that has the breath of life, I have given every green plant for food." And it was so (Gen. 1:28–30).

The two constituent elements in the Dominion Mandate are labor and marriage, or as understood by the ideal young man reading Proverbs, work and wife. Solomon spends time addressing both of them.

All Christians have a mission in life to participate in the Dominion Mandate. What this will look like will vary according to the circumstances of life God has placed you in. If you're a young man, your need for a job or to pursue training in a field isn't merely due to any need for income. It is how God wants you to serve him and others.

Not all men have to work for a living in the same way. A few inherit property that they have to manage while others need to work an hourly job to get food, shelter, and clothing. Many men are called to marriage, but some aren't. All men are called to be stewards of what God has given them, and all men should endeavor to become "marriage material" in their personal character, even if they don't take a wife.

To repeat: From the standpoint of a young male, the Dominion Mandate sets out wife and work as the twin standard of wisdom for adulthood.

So it is no accident that the first section of Proverbs connects choosing wisdom over folly with embracing one's wife and fleeing the adulterous woman. In Genesis 2, we are told that a man must leave his father and mother and cleave to his wife. In Proverbs, Solomon begs his son not only to remember what he has been taught by his parents, but also to discover and embrace Wisdom.

> My son, if you receive my words
>> and treasure up my commandments with you,
> making your ear attentive to wisdom
>> and inclining your heart to understanding;
> yes, if you call out for insight
>> and raise your voice for understanding,
> if you seek it like silver
>> and search for it as for hidden treasures,
> then you will understand the fear of the LORD
>> and find the knowledge of God.
> For the LORD gives wisdom;
>> from his mouth come knowledge and understanding;
> he stores up sound wisdom for the upright;
>> he is a shield to those who walk in integrity,
> guarding the paths of justice
>> and watching over the way of his saints.
> Then you will understand righteousness and justice
>> and equity, every good path;
> for wisdom will come into your heart,
>> and knowledge will be pleasant to your soul;
> discretion will watch over you,

> understanding will guard you,
>> delivering you from the way of evil,
>>> from men of perverted speech,
>> who forsake the paths of uprightness
>>> to walk in the ways of darkness,
>> who rejoice in doing evil
>>> and delight in the perverseness of evil,
>> men whose paths are crooked,
>>> and who are devious in their ways (2:1–15).

Notice the flow here. The father's words and commands are to be "treasured," while wisdom is to be *sought* as if it is hidden treasure ("seek it like silver"). In contrast to what his father is able to give him, only the Lord can give wisdom. Compare this to Proverbs 19:14, "House and wealth are inherited from fathers, but a prudent wife is from the LORD." Just as the man needs to leave home and cleave to his wife, so he also needs to leave childhood, and grow up and cleave to Wisdom. When you are an adult, Wisdom must be a new family member.

> My son, keep my words
>> and treasure up my commandments with you;
> keep my commandments and live;
>> keep my teaching as the apple of your eye;
> bind them on your fingers;
>> write them on the tablet of your heart.
> Say to wisdom, "You are my sister,"
>> and call insight your intimate friend,
> to keep you from the forbidden woman,
>> from the adulteress with her smooth words (7:1–5).

If a son has been raised by godly parents, then they have taught him important truths that he should remember and value. He should never abandon them. But those things are not enough. Like Solomon when he is about to inherit the kingdom, and like Adam needing a companion, every young man becoming an adult needs wisdom from God. He must search for and acquire her.

Thus, Proverbs starts (chs. 1–9) with Solomon exhorting a son to prepare to love his wife (5:15–23), embrace Wisdom, avoid Lady Folly, and evade capture by an adulteress. The book of Proverbs ends (ch. 31) with the Queen Mother telling her son to avoid loose women and to look for a wise wife. That element of the Dominion Mandate is a theme that opens and closes the book. Marriage and wisdom are both involved in being fruitful and multiplying.

We will look more at marriage issues in a later chapter. For now let's look at the other part of the Dominion Mandate.

THE OTHER PERVERSION: DESPISING HONEST WORK

The second component of the Dominion Mandate is also addressed thoroughly in Proverbs: faithful work. While marriage is a special concern in the first and last sections of Proverbs, being a diligent and faithful worker is a major concern throughout. The first temptation to sin that is described in detail in Proverbs is the temptation to be recruited into a gang of murderous bandits who live by plunder (1:8–19). Then the second section or book in Proverbs begins with the same concern:

> The proverbs of Solomon.
> A wise son makes a glad father,
>   but a foolish son is a sorrow to his mother.
> Treasures gained by wickedness do not profit,
>   but righteousness delivers from death.
> The LORD does not let the righteous go hungry,
>   but he thwarts the craving of the wicked.
> A slack hand causes poverty,
>   but the hand of the diligent makes rich.
> He who gathers in summer is a prudent son,
>   but he who sleeps in harvest is a son who brings shame.
> Blessings are on the head of the righteous,
>   but the mouth of the wicked conceals violence (10:1–6).

But it doesn't stop there. The third book, after a general exhortation to wisdom and faith in the true God also warns against theft:

> Incline your ear, and hear the words of the wise....
> Do not rob the poor, because he is poor,
>   or crush the afflicted at the gate,
> for the LORD will plead their cause
>   and rob of life those who rob them (22:17a, 22–23).

The fourth book of Proverbs begins with an exhortation to be impartial in court, but then gives instructions on how to prosper in labor. It is a short book and half of it is about how to work. If the court cases involve property disputes and fraud, then maybe it is all about labor versus pillage:

> These also are sayings of the wise.
> Partiality in judging is not good.
> Whoever says to the wicked, "You are in the right,"
>   will be cursed by peoples, abhorred by nations,
> but those who rebuke the wicked will have delight,
>   and a good blessing will come upon them.
> Whoever gives an honest answer
>   kisses the lips.
> Prepare your work outside;
>   get everything ready for yourself in the field,
>   and after that build your house.
> Be not a witness against your neighbor without cause,
>   and do not deceive with your lips.
> Do not say, "I will do to him as he has done to me;
>   I will pay the man back for what he has done."
> I passed by the field of a sluggard,
>   by the vineyard of a man lacking sense,
> and behold, it was all overgrown with thorns;
>   the ground was covered with nettles,
>   and its stone wall was broken down.
> Then I saw and considered it;
>   I looked and received instruction.
> A little sleep, a little slumber,

a little folding of the hands to rest,
and poverty will come upon you like a robber,
and want like an armed man (24:23–34).

So four out of the seven books of Proverbs appear so concerned with honest labor versus the alternatives that they feature it prominently.

So let's look at the first warning against temptation in Proverbs (1:10–19).

WARNING AGAINST BECOMING A MONSTER

As mentioned above, the two temptations that Solomon describes in detail in the first book of Proverbs are recruitment into a gang of robbers and being enticed by an adulterous wife. These are the two perversions of the Dominion Mandate in Genesis 1, which commissions mankind to work faithfully and to marry faithfully. Furthermore, both temptations revolve around enjoying wealth that belongs to others. This will become obvious when we examine some details in the second warning.

Looking at the first temptation, Solomon argues that it will lead to captivity and death (which is similar to what he said about enjoying another man's wife):

For in vain is a net spread
in the sight of any bird,
but these men lie in wait for their own blood;
they set an ambush for their own lives (1:17–18).

This is a warning that an attempt to gain dominion over others through violence will backfire. One will end up in a situation similar to trapped animals that are ensnared by men for food.

Solomon's argument could be made on the basis of "common sense" (no productive society will put up with violent exploitation forever) or fear of God (he will judge us all). He is probably invoking both lines of reasoning.

But Solomon is also making an additional argument. Consider that the initial temptation is presented as a means of acquiring wealth:

> My son, if sinners entice you,
>   do not consent.
> If they say, "Come with us, let us lie in wait for blood;
>   let us ambush the innocent without reason;
> like Sheol let us swallow them alive,
>   and whole, like those who go down to the pit;
> we shall find all precious goods,
>   we shall fill our houses with plunder;
> throw in your lot among us;
>   we will all have one purse" (1:10–14).

It is important to keep in mind that Solomon does not think a desire for precious goods is evil. He *expects* people to want and pursue such treasure:

- "Whoever is slothful will not roast his game, but the diligent man will get precious wealth" (12:27).

- "Precious treasure and oil are in a wise man's dwelling, but a foolish man devours it" (21:20).

- "By wisdom a house is built, and by understanding it is established; by knowledge the rooms are filled with all precious and pleasant riches" (24:3–4).

The contrast between the foolish and the wise is not that one desires to acquire precious things and the other does not desire to do so. The contrast lies in the means used for attaining them. The tempters present robbery as a shortcut to what will otherwise take diligence, patience, and self-restraint. There is also an element of "luck" involved in acquiring riches, since Proverbs doesn't promise that the wise will always attain wealth or remain wealthy. But the tempters present the rewards of riches as a certainty.

So Solomon's argument is that, however more quickly and certainly you will acquire "precious things" by means of robbery, you will also "acquire," sooner or later, captivity and death.

But there's more to Solomon's warning. When Solomon speaks for the tempters in chapter 1, it is noteworthy that the first thing they mention is murdering the helpless (vv. 11–12), only describing the supposed purpose of the activity afterwards (vv. 13–14). The tempters are revealing something about themselves that Solomon spells out afterwards:

> My son, do not walk in the way with them;
> > hold back your foot from their paths,
> > for their feet run to evil,
> > > and they make haste to shed blood (1:15–16).

Solomon warns against being hasty for wealth (13:11; 20:21; 28:20, 22). But these men are not hasty for riches anymore. They are hasty to kill people! The theft of wealth, that is supposedly the motive for the crime, is really just a rationalization for violence. These people present themselves as engaged in an entrepreneurial venture aimed at profit, but they are really just killers who have found a means of financing their hobby.

Presumably, the son has to be warned about the enticements of these sinners, not because he is looking for an excuse to kill people, but because of his anxieties about making a living at a regular job or impatience with the time it takes to acquire wealth. But if he "makes a living" by plunder, Solomon is warning him that he will grow to enjoy his work.

Later, Solomon elaborates on the process:

> Do not enter the path of the wicked,
> > and do not walk in the way of the evil.
> > Avoid it; do not go on it;

turn away from it and pass on.
For they cannot sleep unless they have done wrong;
    they are robbed of sleep unless they have made someone stumble.
For they eat the bread of wickedness
    and drink the wine of violence.
But the path of the righteous is like the light of dawn,
    which shines brighter and brighter until full day.
The way of the wicked is like deep darkness;
    they do not know over what they stumble (4:14–19).

Wickedness and violence are, to use modern terms, an addiction or a compulsive behavior. A person may begin in a relatively rational manner: He wants good things so much that he takes a seemingly easier and more assured path to them even though it involves sinning against God and other people. But people are "wired" to grow to love what they do, in many instances. Thus, veteran robbers have usually become thrill-seekers. Violence ceases to be a means to an end. It becomes an end in itself.

This argument fits with many other proverbs in the book of Proverbs, as well as the wider context of the Bible.

Human character development works out as Solomon describes because Adam and Eve were intended to grow as servants and rulers by pursuing the Dominion Mandate in a God-pleasing way. Jesus is an example of the principle. Though morally perfect from the beginning, he became a wiser, even "more obedient," person.

- "And the child grew and became strong, filled with wisdom. And the favor of God was upon him" (Luke 2:40).

- "And Jesus increased in wisdom and in stature and in favor with God and man" (Luke 2:52).

- God made Jesus "mature through suffering" (Heb. 2:10b).

- "Although he was a son, he learned obedience through what he suffered. And being made mature..." (Heb. 5:8, 9).

I have translated as "mature" what most translations of Hebrews render in English as "perfect." The traditional translation is misleading to the extent that the same word is not traditionally used in Hebrews 5:14: "But solid food is for the *mature*, for those who have their powers of discernment trained by constant practice to distinguish good from evil."

Jesus pursued his mission according to God's will and, by that process, was changed. Adam and Eve, likewise, were given a mission that would have changed them. Indeed, their mission as God's son and daughter was to become more like God.

Tellingly, the author of Hebrews compares the suffering that his readers must endure to a beloved child maturing under a parent's discipline as Jesus did (Heb. 12:1–11). He explicitly quotes Proverbs 3:11–12. Submitting to God's discipline leads to wisdom and maturity.

WE BECOME WHAT WE DO

The Christian thinker and writer Cornelius Van Til called this process "self-realization" and summarized the mission of Adam and Eve this way:

> That the ethical ideal for man should be self-realization follows from the central place given him in this universe.... Man was to gather up into the prism of his self-conscious activity all the manifold manifestations of the glory of God in order to make one central self-conscious sacrifice of it all to God.
>
> If man was to perform this, his God-given task, he must himself be a fit instrument for this work. He was made a fit instrument for this work, but he must also make himself an ever better instrument for this work. He must will to develop his intellect in order to grasp more comprehensively the wealth of the manifestation of the glory of God in this world. He must will to be an ever better prophet than he already is. He must will to develop his aesthetic capacity, that is, his capacity of appreciation; he must will to be an even better priest than

he already is. Finally, he must will to will the will of God for the whole world; he must become an ever better king than he already is.

For this reason then the primary ethical duty of man is self-realization. Through self-realization man makes himself the king of the earth, and if he is truly the king of the earth then God is truly the king of the universe, since it is as God's creature, as God's vicegerent, that man must seek to develop himself as king. When man becomes truly the king of the universe the kingdom of God is realized, and when the kingdom of God is realized, God is glorified....

But what then, in more detail, is involved in this goal of self-realization that man must set for himself? We can bring this out by working out the idea expressed above, when we said that man must learn to will the will of God. *Man must work out his own will*, that is, he must develop his own will first of all. Man's will needs to become increasingly *spontaneous* in its reactivity. Man was created so that he spontaneously served God. For this reason he must grow in spontaneity. Whatever God has placed within man by way of activity must also be regarded by him as a capacity to be developed. Man was not created merely with a will to will the will of God. In his heart there was an inmost desire to serve God. But just because man was created with this will, God wants man to develop this will.

In the second place, man's will needs to become increasingly *fixed in its self-determination*. In other words, man must needs develop the backbone of his will. Not as though man was created a volitional amoeba, which had to pass through the invertebrate stage before it finally acquired a backbone. Man was created a self. He was the creature of an absolute self and could not be otherwise created than as a self. But for this very reason again man had to develop his self-determination. Man's God is absolutely self-determinate; man will be God-like in proportion that he becomes self-determining and self-determinate under God. In proportion that man develops his self-determination does he develop God's determination or plan for his kingdom on earth. God accomplishes his plans through self-determined characters. An unstable man would be useless in the kingdom of God.

In the third place, man's will must increase in momentum. Man's will would naturally increase in momentum in proportion that it increased in spontaneity and self-determinateness. Yet the point of momentum must be separately mentioned. As man approaches his ideal, the realization of the kingdom of God, the area of his activity naturally enlarges itself. Just as the manager of a growing business needs to increase with his business in alertness, stability, and comprehensiveness of decision, so man, with the development of his progress toward his ideal, would have to develop momentum in order to meet his ever increasing responsibility.[6]

I'm not sure of Van Til's scheme as it relates to prophet, priest, and king, or if his list of different points constitutes different areas of character development rather than different metaphors describing the same thing. But he is undoubtedly right that the *mission given to humanity to transform the world is also a mandate for humans themselves to be transformed into more of God's likeness.* Thus, "the path of the righteous is like the light of dawn, which shines brighter and brighter until full day" (Prov. 4:8).

But Proverbs indicates that the process also works in reverse. To start taking shortcuts or making other perverse decisions, even for permissible ends, will put you on the path to becoming a monster. People who engage in robbery and get away with it for a while will grow to love doing it and to love the sins they have to commit to gain wealth. Your acceptable goals will give way to perverse desires. And those desires will become so powerful that you will find it hard to control them, even when they will obviously cause you harm and risk the things that formerly motivated you to take such actions.

Thus, for example, Solomon isn't optimistic that a person who has developed a violent temper will learn to control it because of negative consequences. The pleasure of anger is a trap for the person who learns to enjoy it:

- "A man of great wrath will pay the penalty, for if you deliver him, you will only have to do it again" (19:19).

- "Make no friendship with a man given to anger, nor go with a wrathful man, lest you learn his ways and entangle yourself in a snare" (22:24–25).

So one of the most basic principles of wisdom is that you can and should train yourself to be wise. And one of the reasons for that obligation is that the only alternative is to train yourself to be a fool.

Living by plunder is the opposite of the Dominion Mandate. Human beings are supposed to provide for themselves by cooperating with each other, not combating one another and confiscating what belongs to others.

◊

Even if you know enough not to embrace a life of robbery, there are other less extreme options that are also foolish and result in obstructing you on your mission in life. Solomon also warns about these, as we will see in the next chapter.

3

THE DERELICTION OF DOMINION

If you can fill the unforgiving minute
With sixty seconds' worth of distance run,
Yours is the Earth and everything that's in it,
And—which is more—you'll be a Man, my son!
  —Rudyard Kipling[7]

Human beings undergo transformations, but they are usually gradual transformations. Parents watching a child grow up may feel that it happened "suddenly." They may talk that way. But usually that expression just means that the changes were so gradual that they didn't pay much attention to them. What was really sudden was when it dawned on them how much their child had changed—that he wasn't really a child now at all. Those small changes accumulate until the parent wakes up to what has been happening.

As I mentioned in the last chapter, Adam and Eve were physical adults when God gave them the Dominion Mandate (Gen. 1:28–30). So as young people move into adulthood the Dominion Mandate becomes much more personally *their* Mandate. But this isn't really a sudden transformation. Various cultures have set the age that begins adulthood differently because that line is somewhat subjective. A boy's development may accelerate, but he doesn't turn into a man overnight except maybe in a legal sense.

Some of the obligations of adulthood precede being a full adult. Some follow after. And each person matures—whether physically, emotionally, or mentally—at his own pace.

So you don't get adult abilities all at once. And, long before you are legally a man, you develop some habits that will empower or hamper you as an adult. Thus, one basic obligation that a youth should take seriously as soon as he is aware of it is to grow in a way that will make him into a better grownup when the time comes.

In other words, even if you're still a child, you are—right now—determining what kind of adult you will be. And you have been doing so for some time. If you are already an adult, you're determining what kind of older adult you will be.

Solomon is telling you how to build a better man. Don't wait for a better time to listen to him.

ROBBERY REPRESENTS MANY OTHER VICES

Solomon begins Proverbs with a vivid description of a temptation a young man can face, the temptation to live by plunder. It is an extreme rejection of the Dominion Mandate that involves dominating and destroying other people rather than subduing the earth. If a youth joins a gang of robbers, there were probably decisions he made earlier in life (or refused to make) that led him to that action. There were habits and attitudes related to work, the use of resources, and respect for others that led him to respond to the offer of living by plunder. Even many of those who would resist a gang's efforts to recruit them haven't made wise decisions or developed good habits. Perhaps they are honest or smart enough not to steal, but they still face problems that stifle their ability to "succeed in life."

Solomon starts with the extreme situation of a criminal gang, but he moves on to other ways young men divert themselves from the Dominion Mandate. Indeed, he begins the second book by mixing up the extreme of plunder with lesser folly:

> Treasures gained by wickedness do not profit,
>> but righteousness delivers from death.
> The LORD does not let the righteous go hungry,
>> but he thwarts the craving of the wicked.
> A slack hand causes poverty,
>> but the hand of the diligent makes rich.
> He who gathers in summer is a prudent son,
>> but he who sleeps in harvest is a son who brings shame.
> Blessings are on the head of the righteous,
>> but the mouth of the wicked conceals violence (10:2–6).

After a general statement about how parents want wise children (v. 1), Solomon revisits the temptation to live by plunder ("treasures gained by wickedness"). Then he mentions other ways a son might become foolish rather than wise in relation to productivity.

SLEEP: BLESSING OR CURSE?

> How long will you lie there, O sluggard?
>> When will you arise from your sleep?
> A little sleep, a little slumber,
>> a little folding of the hands to rest,
> and poverty will come upon you like a robber,
>> and want like an armed man.
> — Prov. 6:9–11; see also 24:33–34

In the Bible, sleep is a means of refreshment but also a time of vulnerability to disaster because one is oblivious to threats. We might say there is resurrection sleep and death sleep. Adam was put to sleep so he could be given Eve (Gen. 2). Abram was put to sleep to receive God's covenant (Gen. 15). But the Canaanite general Sisera was lured to sleep to be assassinated (Judg. 9). Notice that Solomon is taking that vulnerability to hostile attack as a metaphor for how sleep can be a problem. As Sisera was slain by Jael and her tent peg, so you risk being defeated by poverty if you sleep too much.

So, in later Scripture, we get sleep as a curse rather than a blessing from God.

> Astonish yourselves and be astonished;
>> blind yourselves and be blind!
> Be drunk, but not with wine;
>> stagger, but not with strong drink!
> For the LORD has poured out upon you
>> a spirit of deep sleep,
> and has closed your eyes (the prophets),
>> and covered your heads (the seers) (Isa. 29:9–10).

> They shall roar together like lions;
>> they shall growl like lions' cubs.
> While they are inflamed I will prepare them a feast
>> and make them drunk, that they may become merry,
> then sleep a perpetual sleep
>> and not wake, declares the LORD.
> I will bring them down like lambs to the slaughter,
>> like rams and male goats (Jer. 51:38–40).

So prosperity will lead to "sleep," which will mean vulnerability to destruction.

Then, in the synoptic Gospels, we have the issue of sleep in the garden of Gethsemane. Jesus rebuked Peter, James, and John because they fell asleep when they were supposed to pray.

The Apostle Paul appeals to the same theme in his letter to the Romans:

> Besides this you know the time, that the hour has come for you to wake from sleep. For salvation is nearer to us now than when we first believed. The night is far gone; the day is at hand. So then let us cast off the works of darkness and put on the armor of light. Let us walk properly as in the daytime,

not in orgies and drunkenness, not in sexual immorality and sensuality, not in quarreling and jealousy. But put on the Lord Jesus Christ, and make no provision for the flesh, to gratify its desires (13:11–14).

Thus, while sleep can be refreshing and good (Prov. 3:24), it also can entail a lack of awareness or concern. People "fall asleep" to righteousness and so fall into unrighteousness and ultimately also self-destructive behavior.

But while we have a theme that runs through much of Scripture, it appears only rarely in any passage from before Solomon.

Isn't that strange? Solomon says things like "Slothfulness casts into a deep sleep, and an idle person will suffer hunger" (Prov. 19:15). Moses doesn't say anything about the danger of sleep, but Solomon can't shut up about it.

And sleep isn't the only thing that Solomon warns against more than Moses did.

STRONG DRINK, WEAK MEN

Similarly, Solomon obsesses over getting drunk. We don't have any official commands against drunkenness until the time of Solomon. In fact, quite the opposite: alcohol is commended:

> You shall tithe all the yield of your seed that comes from the field year by year. And before the LORD your God, in the place that he will choose, to make his name dwell there, you shall eat the tithe of your grain, of your wine, and of your oil, and the firstborn of your herd and flock, that you may learn to fear the LORD your God always. And if the way is too long for you, so that you are not able to carry the tithe, when the LORD your God blesses you, because the place is too far from you, which the LORD your God chooses, to set his name there, then you shall turn it into money and bind up the money in your hand and go to the place that the LORD your God chooses and spend the money for whatever you desire—oxen or sheep

or wine or strong drink, whatever your appetite craves. And you shall eat there before the LORD your God and rejoice, you and your household. And you shall not neglect the Levite who is within your towns, for he has no portion or inheritance with you (Deut. 14:22–27).

Obviously, Moses presents "strong drink" as a blessing, but it is worth noting that he describes it when used as part of a celebration and an official rest from a time of labor. While on duty, the priest and Levites serving in God's house were not allowed to drink (Lev. 10:9). From the rule to the priests, we can infer that drinking should not interfere with work and that there will be consequences if a person allows it to do so. Furthermore, the stories of Noah (Gen. 9:20ff.) and Lot (19:30ff.) show us also that drinking excessively leaves a person vulnerable to exploitation.

Additionally, we are told that a typical "professional" criminal will be "a drunkard and a glutton" (Deut. 21:18–21). This passage is commonly misunderstood as some kind of death penalty for children, but it really is a demand that parents turn evidence against habitual offenders of serious crimes—adult crimes. The language of the passage is reminiscent of Proverbs 1, and it assumes that someone who is uninterested in honest work will seek a life of theft and fraud by a desire to consume food and alcoholic beverages. The implication is that the criminal is focused on consumption rather than production.

Prior to Solomon, the Scriptures might lead us to the conclusion that alcohol can be abused, but we don't have statements from Genesis through Judges like this: "Wine is a mocker, strong drink a brawler, and whoever is led astray by it is not wise" (Prov. 20:1). We get even longer, more descriptive warnings in Proverbs 23:29–34 and Proverbs 31:4–9. Drunkenness is barely mentioned by Moses, but Solomon obsesses over it. Notice that Solomon doesn't disagree with Moses. He too thinks that wine is a blessing (Prov. 3:2, 9:2, 5). But he spends more time warning about abusing alcohol than Moses does.

As with the case of warnings against sleep, we have to ask ourselves the reason for this change.

PROSPERITY IS A TEST AND A THREAT

We are told that Solomon, at the height of his reign, "made silver as common in Jerusalem as stone, and he made cedar as plentiful as the sycamore of the Shephelah" (1 Kgs. 10:27). In Proverbs, we're seeing the fruits of meditating on the Law of Moses as well as the Word of God expressed for a more prosperous and urban people. Up until a generation earlier, Israel has been an agriculture-based confederation of tribes. Agriculture is still important, but now Israel is a wealthy kingdom that is centered on a major city. Israel is richer and has more of an international reach. There are ways to provide for oneself on business trips rather than by simply planting crops or herding cattle (the husband in Prov. 7). A mother is no longer tied to the family farm to feed her family but "brings her food from afar" (Prov. 31:14).

So now something that has always been true becomes a more pressing concern. People have always needed to be diligent workers. In the Ten Commandments given from Mount Sinai, the Fourth Commandment describes work as essential, telling people to work six days and rest on the seventh. But it is likely that neglecting the farm for a life of drunkenness was more immediately punished. Not only would you experience consequences within a year—the failure to plant means there won't be a crop—but if you were still living at home, your father would make you regret your negligence.

But with economic opportunity comes geographic mobility and an extended time frame. With more wealth in society, young men are more likely to be able to spend money on wine and strong drink and experiment with making it a regular habit. They also may be able to afford to stay out all night and quit their jobs without notice in order to sleep in, on the assumption that they can always pick up new ones.

In other words, when it is an obvious struggle to survive and you live or die by the rain and other factors, the principles of staving off death are more easily understood, at least for people who know the basic commands of God. But when you have more wealth in society you have the increasing possibility of young men and women growing up thinking they are entitled. Poverty and disaster seem like distant concerns, not real threats that require diligence to escape in life.

Consider the Prodigal Son (Luke 15:11–32). He did not simply plan to spend all his money and then starve. Jesus makes a point in telling us that a famine arose. A massive ongoing food shortage would have made prices rise and caused other economic hardships. A wise person prepares for future contingencies as much as possible so he can "laugh at the time to come" (Prov. 31:25), but the Prodigal assumed that nothing would disrupt the good times of plenty. He didn't plan for emergencies. As crazy as it seems, prosperity can bring about poverty because people allow themselves to become useless—skilled at consuming resources but unable to produce wealth.

So when Solomon warns repeatedly of the dangers of sleep and alcohol (and sloth and rich, adulterous wives, etc.), he is telling such people to "wake up." There is now immense new potential for young people to live better than their fathers, but they still need to pay attention to their lives. It is dangerous to assume that you can sleep-walk through life and expect everything to come out all right. "Love not sleep, lest you come to poverty; open your eyes, and you will have plenty of bread" (Prov. 20:13).

It bears repeating that, as damaging as heavy drinking ("alcoholism") can be, in Proverbs it is one of many bad habits that can weaken you and even destroy you. Bad habits of overdulging in things that are (initially) pleasant are hard to break and obstruct your ability to accomplish anything worthwhile. So while you should avoid becoming an alcoholic, you should avoid other vices as well. They all will lead to death if they get the upper hand.

YOU CAN'T ESCAPE REALITY

Solomon writes, "He who gathers in summer is a prudent son, but he who sleeps in harvest is a son who brings shame" (Prov. 10:5). I doubt anyone growing up on a farm would need to be told that. A missed harvest would mean immediate pain. Solomon's point is that young men growing up in Jerusalem haven't left reality behind.

Youths who have left the farm for the city still have to be productive or they will regret the results. Even in relative prosperity, negligence can have serious consequences. The fact that these consequences are delayed makes them worse. People adapt to what they do. They are changed by their behavior. So when a young man grows to love sleep or alcohol or some other excess, he has a much harder time changing his behavior when he gets older. Such change often seems unthinkable and it is always difficult. Even if he is successful, he has passed by opportunities that he will never get back. Regrets are also burdensome.

This is especially relevant to our own age. Incredible wealth, especially in the form of technology that provides relief from labor, is unquestionably a great blessing from God and the fruit of generations of Christian progress. It is a far greater economic transformation than what happened in Israel under Saul, David, and Solomon. But it seems our prosperity has made possible a great deal of the preposterous confidence throughout society that we can dispense with biblical guidelines. A great deal of our society's rejection of the Bible's rules for sex and the family can be traced to this new wealth. Many of the absurd economic promises made by politicians make sense only among a population that takes wealth for granted and doesn't think it is difficult to produce.

But wealth still must be created by productive labor and children are still produced by (and only by) pairings of a man and a woman. Reproduction still sidelines women far more than men from other economic endeavors, despite the attempts of regimes and CEOs to use resources to equalize the situation. The biology of the sexes hasn't fundamentally changed, though technology has helped sell such a fantasy. Likewise, people who consume more than they produce are only going to become poorer and debt can only make such a situation worse.

Solomon reminds us that we are not angels but animals—made in God's image but as biological creatures. We haven't transcended nature nor discovered a magic spell which makes wealth appear out of nothing. Primal realities may be less onerous in a prosperous society, but they never disappear.

Falling asleep to reality will not end well.

A SLUGGARD CANNOT RULE WELL

The overarching habit which includes oversleep and drunkenness and many other vices is sloth. The virtue opposite of sloth is *diligence.*

> The hand of the diligent will rule,
> while the slothful will be put to forced labor....
> Whoever is slothful will not roast his game,
> but the diligent man will get precious wealth.
> In the path of righteousness is life,
> and in its pathway there is no death (Prov. 12:24, 27–28).

Men and women are meant to reflect God's glory by working and transforming creation as well as by uniting in marriage to spread that work of transformation through generations. The Dominion Mandate defines who we as human beings *are.* To the extent we resist and distort that calling, we damage ourselves. There are many different ways to fulfill the Mandate. Some people farm, others serve for an hourly wage, while others manage an inheritance. But this is the design and plan for the human race as a whole.

Thus, because God made us to take possession of the world by our efforts, Solomon has to warn young men (and everyone else) against sloth.

Some marginalize this part of Scripture as "law" versus "gospel," or as Old Testament moralism, or as insignificant compared to other parts of the Bible. Don't do that. Remember that what we do is who we become.

As we saw in the last chapter, Adam and Eve, in subduing and ruling over the earth in fact and not only in title, would pretty obviously also come to rule themselves in a new and more complete way. And each person, as he or she grew up and participated in the royal project, would be transformed into a new kind of king or queen.

That's our story and our identity. We were derailed from that track by sin but in Christ we are back on course.

When King Solomon seeks to teach us about how to grow up and become strong, filled with wisdom just as Jesus was (Luke 2:40), he has to warn us about what would weaken us, warp our growth, and ultimately dehumanize us.

Loving Leisure Leads to Slavery

In a way, it's quite natural. We all enjoy leisure. There is nothing wrong with that. But like anything else, we may not be able to have as much as we want as soon as we want. We can mess up our lives if we can't resist the desire for leisure in order to get what we need. "The desire of the sluggard kills him, for his hands refuse to labor" (Prov. 21:25).

Notice the desire is treated as an external threat that attacks a person. Why?

Because the person isn't acting like an integrated, mature adult. Everyone desires leisure, but they also desire to be able to have some reasonable chance to provide for themselves and others in the future. They also want to be able to take pride in their accomplishments. Somehow, the desire for relief from work overcomes these other things. A person develops bad habits and fails to develop good ones. These habits obstruct a youth from growing into the great man he is supposed to become. So the attitude or habit or appetite is a threat to a person's best interests. The desire can become an attacker that can hurt, trap, and destroy a person's life.

And the desire will provide plausible rationalizations. "The sluggard does not plow in the autumn; he will seek at harvest and have nothing" (Prov. 20:4). Well, who wants to work outside when it's wet and cold?

Or the desire will cultivate in us real fears that intimidate us, even though the things that intimidate us are not as risky as the sloth that they justify. "The sluggard says, 'There is a lion outside! I shall be killed in the streets!'" (22:13). Well, maybe. It is always possible that if you go to work or school tomorrow morning you might be injured or killed. Stranger things have happened.

But that is not a rational way to live. The odds are, if you suffer from such fears, you already don't want to go outside for other reasons. You're thinking of things that might go wrong because you want an excuse. So instead of being a courageous king, you are enslaved by anxieties.

Often, if we go down this path, we become resistant to people who want to talk us out of our cherished illusions: "The sluggard is wiser in his own eyes than seven men who can answer sensibly" (26:16).

Sometimes people are willing to work, but only for a little while before they quit. Thus, the opposite of sloth isn't "hard work" necessarily. Nor is it even "long hours." Someone might boast in working long hours three days a month when the project requires more consistent, dedicated time than that. Long hours are necessitated in certain circumstances but not all. That is why the antithesis of sloth is consistency or *diligence*. Diligence is contrasted with sloth more than once in the book of Proverbs. Sloth will begin but not end a task. "Whoever is slothful will not roast his game, but the diligent man will get precious wealth" (12:27). So he'll go through the effort of hunting but not bother to cook—defeating the point of hunting in the first place.

"The sluggard buries his hand in the dish and will not even bring it back to his mouth" (19:24). This ridiculous image emphasizes the point. People start something, then get impatient and discouraged and quit before they should. While sometimes a sluggard might not plant, often he does plant but doesn't bother to harvest: "He who gathers in summer is a prudent son, but he who sleeps in harvest is a son who brings shame" (10:5). All the previous work is undone by later slothfulness.

RISK AND REWARD

Since sloth is the opposite of diligence, it can be characterized both by a lack of ambition and by an unrealistic expectation of quick wealth. "The plans of the diligent lead surely to abundance, but everyone who is hasty comes only to poverty" (Prov. 21:5). In general, we need to be careful of shortcuts and schemes that offer us things we should know are too good to be true, because there's something in us that wants to believe false promises that are likely to fail. "Whoever works his land will have plenty of bread, but he who follows worthless pursuits will have plenty of poverty" (28:19; see also 12:11).

This resistance to high-risk, allegedly high-reward schemes on the part of the wise may explain some of the seemingly contradictory sayings in Proverbs. Consider these two:

- "The prudent sees danger and hides himself, but the simple go on and suffer for it" (27:12).

- "The wicked flee when no one pursues, but the righteous are bold as a lion" (28:1).

Obviously these have to be applied differently, but it seems that the prudent are less likely to pursue these hasty schemes while the sluggard embraces them. The youths who join a bandits' gang are ignoring the danger they are in. On the other hand, being diligent involves confidence and faith that God will take care of you. Others let their fears put them at risk of impoverishment. They fear "the lion outside" that may not even exist.

So embracing diligence and avoiding sloth means being ruled neither by anxieties and fears nor by dreams and fantasies.

◊

One of the worst rationalizations of slothfulness is the assumption that anyone who wants you to work (parent, teacher, employer) is like an enemy slave driver. We'll deal with this more in the next chapter. But here is the main point: God wants you to be strong, not weak!

God's rules and God's wisdom are aimed at empowering you to make you capable of doing great things. Adam and Eve ruined their lives because they decided that God was trying to keep them down. The path of disobedience appeared to them to be the path of freedom. But it was entirely the other way around. The path of disobedience was completely scripted by Satan and they were allowing themselves to be manipulated by the serpent.

God wants to elevate you. The moment you let yourself think that his rules are an impediment to you rather than a way of unleashing your potential, you are a fool.

4

FIGHTING FOR THE FUTURE

I have heard that nothing gives an author so great pleasure, as to find his works respectfully quoted by others. Judge, then, how much I must have been gratified by an incident I am going to relate to you.

I stopped my horse, lately, where a great number of people were collected at an auction of merchants' goods. The hour of the sale not being come, they were conversing on the badness of the times; and one of the company called to a plain, clean, old man, with white locks, "Pray, Father Abraham, what think you of the times? Will not those heavy taxes quite ruin the country! How shall we be ever able to pay them? What would you advise us to?"——Father Abraham stood up, and replied, "If you would have my advice, I will give it you in short; 'for a word to the wise is enough,' as Poor Richard says." They joined in desiring him to speak his mind, and, gathering round him, he proceeded as follows:

"Friends," says he, "the taxes are indeed very heavy; and, if those laid on by the government were the only ones we had to pay, we might more easily discharge them; but we have many others, and much more grievous to some of us. We are taxed twice as much by our idleness, three times as much by our pride, and four times as much by our folly; and from these taxes the commissioners cannot ease or deliver us by allowing an abatement."

—Benjamin Franklin[8]

Wisdom is intimately related to preparing for the future, or future possibilities, in the present.

For example, in Matthew's Gospel, the first parable Jesus tells related to wisdom is the story of the two builders and their two houses (Matt. 7:24– 27). The last parable mentioning wisdom is about the virgins waiting for the bridegroom (Matt. 25:1–13). In the first story, the fool builds his house on sand while the wise man builds on the rock. The fool's house is destroyed in a storm while the house on the rock remains standing. In the last story, half of the ten virgins (deemed "foolish") did not bring enough oil to keep their lamps lit for a long time. When the bridegroom arrived later than expected—at midnight—they had already burned all their oil.

And the foolish said to the wise, "Give us some of your oil, for our lamps are going out." But the wise answered, saying, "Since there will not be enough for us and for you, go rather to the dealers and buy for yourselves." And while they were going to buy, the bridegroom came, and those who were ready went in with him to the marriage feast, and the door was shut. Afterward the other virgins came also, saying, "Lord, lord, open to us." But he answered, "Truly, I say to you, I do not know you." Watch therefore, for you know neither the day nor the hour (Matt. 25:8–13).

In both these cases, the wise were the ones who planned for future contingencies. Planning for unending sunny days is called "not planning." Jesus doesn't say anything about the work ethic of the builders. We're not told that one was lazy and another was a hard worker. Presumably both used hired help. But their planning reflected different character traits. Sloth isn't just about whether you will work at physical tasks of labor, but whether you will think about reality rather than act according to wishful thinking. Consider these two passages in Proverbs:

> I passed by the field of a sluggard,
>> by the vineyard of a man lacking sense,
> and behold, it was all overgrown with thorns;
>> the ground was covered with nettles,
>> and its stone wall was broken down.
> Then I saw and considered it;
>> I looked and received instruction.
> A little sleep, a little slumber,
>> a little folding of the hands to rest,
> and poverty will come upon you like a robber,
>> and want like an armed man (24:30–34).

> Know well the condition of your flocks,
>> and give attention to your herds,
> for riches do not last forever;
>> and does a crown endure to all generations?
> When the grass is gone and the new growth appears
>> and the vegetation of the mountains is gathered,
> the lambs will provide your clothing,
>> and the goats the price of a field.
> There will be enough goats' milk for your food,
>> for the food of your household
>> and maintenance for your girls (27:23–27).

As I mentioned in the last chapter, "sleep" isn't always meant literally. No one sleeps long enough to have his field become a ruin. But one might "sleep" to reality by not bothering to "know well the condition" of his resources or "give attention" to the risks and liabilities he faces. Thus, being a sluggard isn't necessarily about manual labor. Both these passages would apply to a wealthy man with servants. Slothfulness can be mental, a refusal to face reality and plan accordingly. Thus, a sluggard is a person "lacking sense."

It may seem odd for a book affirming that only God knows the future should condemn a lack of foresight, but God wants us to grow up into trustworthy managers who pay attention to what he is doing rather than escape into wishful thinking. God has made the real world, the only one in which we live, prone to unforeseen but not entirely unexpected hardships. Whether famines or economic recessions, illnesses or accidents, people run into emergencies that reduce income, rob their time, and force them to spend money.

There is a form of ungodly optimism that should be contrasted with the godly optimism of faith in the true God. This antithesis goes back to the temptation in the garden of Eden where the serpent's prediction about the future was contrasted with God's warning. If a person is content to live "hand to mouth," paycheck to paycheck, in a world where problems disrupt the lives of others around him, he is presuming to live a charmed life. He is the man building his house on the sand. He is the virgin who didn't bother to bring extra oil for her lamp.

God doesn't condemn people for not guessing correctly. In Jesus' parables, the wrong decisions he addresses are not simple mistakes about the future. They are foolish refusals to think about the future and baseless presumptions that all will be well.

On the other hand, God promises to bless wisdom and diligence. "The soul of the sluggard craves and gets nothing, while the soul of the diligent is richly supplied" (Prov. 13:4). We should be generally optimistic that, if we do what we reasonably can to protect ourselves, wisdom will pay off. That is, of course, a generalization. But even when there is an exceptional emergency or disaster, at least you will have the satisfaction of knowing you weren't vulnerable to it by your own foolishness.

C. S. Lewis talked about a similar kind of foolish wishful thinking when he wrote about those who asked if it was possible to be a good person without affirming Christian doctrine. The person asking this question knew what the Christian faith asserted and was not denying that it *might* be true. So Lewis writes:

> He is really asking, "Need I bother about it? Mayn't I just evade the issue, just let sleeping dogs lie, and get on with being "good"? Aren't good intentions enough to keep me safe and blameless without knocking at that dreadful door and making sure whether there is, or isn't, someone inside?
>
> To such a man it might be enough to reply that he is really asking to be allowed to get on with being "good" before he has done his best to discover what *good* means. But that is not the whole story.... The man is shirking. He is deliberately trying not to know whether Christianity is true or false, because he foresees endless trouble if it should turn out to be true. He is like the man who deliberately "forgets" to look at the notice board because, if he did, he might find his name down for some unpleasant duty. He is like the man who won't look at his bank account because he's afraid of what he might find there. He is like the man who won't go to the doctor when he first feels a mysterious pain because he is afraid of what the doctor may tell him.
>
> The man who remains an unbeliever for such reasons is not in a state of honest error. He is in a state of dishonest error, and that dishonesty will spread through all his thoughts and actions: a certain shiftiness, a vague worry in the back-ground, a blunting of his whole mental edge, will result.[9]

Slothfulness in our thinking is a foolish shirking of our responsibilities that leads to bad consequences in the future. Foolishness leads to more foolishness, and wishful thinking keeps a person from protecting himself from harm. As Wisdom says, "the complacency of fools destroys them" (Prov. 1:31).

This habit of refusing to think accurately about reality is both a form of sloth itself and a mental habit that develops from the more physical habit of sloth. After all, the only way to be content as a sluggard is to pretend one won't be damaged by one's behavior. Slothfulness of hand becomes slothfulness of head and heart.

Thus, when it focuses on diligence in working, Proverbs includes the diligence of saving for the future.

Handguns Can't Shoot Down Poverty

Should a young man buy a handgun?

This is a controversial question in American political culture right now. Some strongly advocate for legal restrictions on gun ownership and possession. Others strongly favor the restriction of the legislature and the rest of civil government to the dictates of the Second Amendment in the U.S. Bill of Rights. As they see it, an armed populace is ultimately safer from crimes and can't be controlled as easily by domestic or foreign governments.

But even if a young man believes in the Second Amendment in this way, it may be a stupid decision to purchase a gun. His thinking may be clouded with slogans and visions from action movies rather than by a sober evaluation of his actual circumstances and risks.

My argument for this is simple and two-fold. The first reason is that handguns are expensive to purchase and also expensive to keep since practice with them requires the cost of ammunition and usually a designated place. The second reason is more important and universal: A growing stash of saved wealth is usually the main tool of personal freedom and independence, not a handgun.

- "Whoever loves pleasure will be a poor man; he who loves wine and oil will not be rich" (Prov. 21:17).

- "Precious treasure and oil are in a wise man's dwelling, but a foolish man devours it" (Prov. 21:20).

Undoubtedly there are circumstances where a handgun—along with discipline and proficiency in using it—is more valuable than all the money in the world at that particular moment. But much of the entertainment industry is concentrated on people facing such scenarios, making them seem common. Outside of fantasy entertainment, those circumstances are quite rare for virtually anyone who is reading these words. As far as "resistance to tyranny" goes, the government has its citizens outgunned. Practically speaking, after staying out of trouble altogether, the most important tool one can possess in dealing with government hostility in the U.S. is the ability to afford a skillful lawyer.

The most common villain every person faces throughout all the world and all history is poverty. It is a "robber" and an "armed man" (Prov. 6:11; 24:34). This is true even in affluent societies. Financial emergencies and setbacks, personal and societal, are a hazard of life. Thus, the most important weapon to defeat that villain is a growing stash of cash and/or an expanding bank account and/or an increasing collection of assets designed to produce income or at least be liquidated (not things you acquire to enjoy directly and thus make them less valuable, but things you acquire to sell or make money from). If, while gaining this sort of weapon, you believe it can be helpful to own a handgun and that you can do so responsibly, go ahead. But without amassing some wealth, purchasing something so impractical and expensive is stupid.

The fantasy of needing to be able to deal with an armed opponent can distract you from the real threat you face. The Second Amendment's vision of human life may be true, but that doesn't make a young man's decision to purchase a handgun wise. Being distracted into giving up money you will probably need to acquire something you probably won't need is irrational.

- "The discerning sets his face toward wisdom, but the eyes of a fool are on the ends of the earth" (Prov. 17:24).

- "Whoever works his land will have plenty of bread, but he who follows worthless pursuits lacks sense" (Prov. 12:11).

If you are dependent on and responsible for a car, for example, the ability to repair or replace it is probably a more pressing need than combating hostiles who have taken over Nakatomi Plaza.

The problem is that one either gets in the habit of saving money or spending money. Many people get set in this habit at an early age. If you have the wrong habit, it is human nature to accept it as normative and rationalize it. Instead of figuring out what is the best way to live, we utilize all our brain power to justify what we have already been doing.

When many American teens get jobs, they do so to buy things they want over and above what their parents are willing to spend on them. This seems responsible but it means they get habituated to earning money for things they want to purchase and use immediately. That habit is insufficient for productive life as an adult.

Many people realize they need to save and assume they will change their behavior when they get a "real job." But a lot of people find that the "real job" barely covers real expenses. Unless they've already cultivated the habit of saving money, it will be very difficult to change their behavior. It is much better to have already developed an obsession to save rather than an obsession to have things you don't need at the expense of saving. You need to get to the point where depleting your savings causes as much mental pain as not having some luxury you want.

As always, God wants us to be wise in order to empower us. Nothing in Proverbs indicates that it's actually wrong to acquire and enjoy luxuries. But that enjoyment needs to be done in a way that doesn't sabotage you as a person and rob you of financial freedom.

DEBT AND DEAFNESS TO WISDOM

If Proverbs teaches that saving is a basic practice and habit of wise living, then going into debt when you don't have to is doubly foolish. Solomon spends time giving an example of the importance of getting out of debt.

> My son, if you have put up security for your neighbor,
>   have given your pledge for a stranger,
> if you are snared in the words of your mouth,
>   caught in the words of your mouth,
> then do this, my son, and save yourself,
>   for you have come into the hand of your neighbor:
>   go, hasten, and plead urgently with your neighbor.
> Give your eyes no sleep
>   and your eyelids no slumber;
> save yourself like a gazelle from the hand of the hunter,
>   like a bird from the hand of the fowler (6:1–5).

Notice that of all the situations Solomon chooses to address, he picks cosigning for a charitable loan. If anything could be justified you would think it would be helping out someone else. But no. Solomon compares someone who cosigns a loan to a trapped animal who needs to escape if at all possible. This is the same metaphor Solomon uses for people who attempt to live by violent plunder or allow themselves to be seduced by an adulteress. It is an image that goes back to Genesis and the design of men and women to have dominion over the animals. To be like a trapped animal is a degradation of a human being.

Debt is not a sin. Proverbs explains, "The rich rules over the poor, and the borrower is the slave of the lender" (22:7). It's not a sin to be poor and it's not a sin to be forced into debt. But it is sinful folly to develop habits that lead you into poverty, and going into debt is one of the shortest paths to that destination.

> Be not one of those who give pledges,
>   who put up security for debts.

If you have nothing with which to pay,
>   why should your bed be taken from under you? (22:26–27)

Developing the habit of consuming less than you produce and saving the excess helps you to avoid debt. And debt is the reverse of saving. Saving makes you less financially vulnerable. Debt does the opposite.

Even in biblical times when there wasn't nearly the wealth we have now, Solomon recognized that the poverty caused by human folly at least matched the scarcity God imposed when he cursed the earth because of sin. Remember, God told Adam that the punishment for sin would be difficulty in getting food. "Cursed is the ground because of you; in pain you shall eat of it all the days of your life; thorns and thistles it shall bring forth for you" (Gen. 3: 17b–18a). Yet Proverbs teaches that slothful habits are their own punishment. "The way of a sluggard is like a hedge of thorns, but the path of the upright is a level highway" (Prov. 15:19). People create their own thorns and thistles over and above anything God has done in response to human sin.

Taking on avoidable debt means you have to be diligent to recover your life rather than increasing what you have. You are forced to spend your days filling up a hole rather than building anything new.

Since the Bible doesn't say it is a sin, in itself, to go into debt—just like it is not a sin to be poor—I won't say so either. If or when one should take on debt is a discussion outside the scope of this book. But there is no point to read and consider the arguments of others unless you have become a habitual saver and debt-avoider. Otherwise, you are going to be looking for excuses to be able to spend more than you make. Those excuses are "richly supplied" by people who wish to make money by loaning to you. "The simple believes everything, but the prudent gives thought to his steps" (Prov. 14:15).

This touches on a point mentioned in the last chapter. It is very easy for a person to gravitate toward people who encourage wishful thinking. Thus, a young man doesn't usually like to be told that he needs to spend less time playing video games and more time studying. Likewise, no one wants to hear that he needs to cut expenses or that a car is out of his reach because he shouldn't take out a loan to get it. But there are plenty of people who say what you do want to hear—especially car salesmen and the video game industry. It is quite common for people—of every age—to listen to those who tell them what they want to hear and treat what such people say as a rational basis for their decisions. But what is really happening is that they have already made their decision and are listening to the voices that side with them to drown out wiser advice.

Your parents and others are probably not telling you things they know you don't want to hear in order to ruin your fun. They are saying things that will lead to your empowerment and prosperity. When you go searching for other sources of (dis)information to use to argue against them, are you being rational or stubborn? If thinking is a good thing to do, then you owe it to yourself to think about your own thinking. Are you being rational or merely rationalizing wishful thinking? Are you really listening *carefully* to what is being said?

People often associate crime or vice with low intelligence. After all, how can it be smart to suffer deprivation or fall into debt just because you want a "cool" smart phone that lets you buy things with a facial expression? But that fails to account for the powerful desire people have to justify their behavior. Once a bad habit starts, smart people will be prone to use all their brain power for making the habit seem virtuous. That's why we read more than once the plea and warning "do not be wise in you own eyes" (Prov. 3:7; 16:2; 21:2; 12:12; Isa. 5:21; Rom. 12:16; see also Prov. 14:12; 16:25). While searching for people to confirm what you want may be framed as searching for counsel, it is actually a way to ignore wisdom. "The way of a fool is right in his own eyes, but a wise man listens to advice" (Prov. 12:15).

Sloth Degrades Everything, Even Spirituality

Avoiding and killing sloth may or may not lead to economic success. It will definitely leave you better off than you would be otherwise. But in absolute terms no one can promise how your future will turn out. Contrary to popular opinion in some circles, it simply isn't true that Solomon thinks the wise always get rich and the foolish always get poor. Solomon considers wisdom as preferable to all other wealth. Sometimes wisdom and wealth don't coincide. Wisdom and personal character, however, do coincide. (I will discuss this in more detail in chapter 8.)

The issues of diligence and sloth are used by Jesus to illustrate the basics of living the Christian life. Consider his parable in Matthew 25:

> Now after a long time the master of those servants came and settled accounts with them. And he who had received the five talents came forward, bringing five talents more, saying, "Master, you delivered to me five talents; here, I have made five talents more." His master said to him, "Well done, good and faithful servant. You have been faithful over a little; I will set you over much. Enter into the joy of your master."

At a certain level, slothfulness translates into unbelief and faith in Jesus Christ is displayed as diligence. Thus, the Apostle Paul writes:

> And let us *not grow weary of doing good*, for in due season we will reap, if we do not give up. So then, as we have opportunity, let us do good to everyone, and especially to those who are of the household of faith (Gal. 6:9–10).

How could one follow Paul's instructions in Romans 12 without developing diligence and therefore avoiding sloth? "*Do not be slothful in zeal*, be fervent in spirit, serve the Lord. Rejoice in hope, be patient in tribulation, be constant in prayer" (Rom. 12:11–12).

So these are things God wants us to work on, promising to help us. In so doing, he gets us to work on ourselves and the kind of people we are becoming. Patient diligence in work and patient saving for the future improve our ability to trust God in daily life. And faith in God, in turn, motivates us to be diligent. Bad habits creep into everyone's behavior, but when you notice them you have an opportunity to begin to change for the better.

SLOTH IS A VICE AND ALL VICES ARE SLOTH

Reportedly, there was a saying among early colonial Christians in New England: "Idle hands are the Devil's workshop." In other words, if you are being slothful you are leaving yourself open to temptation to sin. But there's another way of looking about how these things are related. We could accurately reverse the saying: "The Devil's workshop produces idle hands (and empty savings accounts)." Sloth doesn't just make us vulnerable to vices, but vices make us slothful in doing any good as well.

God doesn't want us to sin, but there's more to what God wants than us abstaining from a series of behaviors he prohibits. Positively, God created the human race to be masters of the universe. He wanted an expanding army of diligent workers. When a sin gets dominion over our life in some way, we not only do what's wrong, but we also neglect to do what's right. Solomon sometimes describes sins not for their perversity but for how they impoverish us. An example from Proverbs: "He who loves wisdom makes his father glad, but a companion of prostitutes squanders his wealth" (29:3).

Thus, if the Devil wants to frustrate God's will for the world, he may be encouraging vices to spread throughout society not only for the sake of promoting sin but to promote weakness and reduced productivity among Christians. He wants us to be slothful rather than diligent. And vices are an effective way to sideline Christians so that much of their time, energy, and wealth is siphoned from things they could be accomplishing if they were able to focus on goals.

God, on the contrary, wants us to be persevering, goal-oriented transformers of the world. In becoming such people we increasingly reflect his glory. "Therefore, since we have so great a cloud of witnesses surrounding us, let us also lay aside every encumbrance and the sin which so easily entangles us, and let us run with endurance the race that is set before us..." (Heb. 12:1 NASB).

5

IMMORALITY IMPOVERISHES YOU

...for nothing is better than this, more steadfast than when two people, a man and his wife, keep a harmonious household; a thing that brings much distress to the people who hate them.

—Homer, *The Odyssey*[10]

The Dominion Mandate that God gave Adam and Eve centers on productive labor and marriage. To restate the point: from the standpoint of a young man, it is about work and wife. Since the first two temptations Solomon spells out in great detail are living by murder and plunder (ch. 1) and adultery (ch. 7), we can say that the alternative to dominion is sex and violence (referring, of course, to fornication and aggression with related vices, not marriage and self-defense). We've talked about robbery and its parent, sloth. Now we need to address illicit sex.

◊

"Family values" is a slogan for many Christians. For some people, the term indicates that the values that originate in the family are the values that should govern all of the society. If this means simply heterosexual monogamy being the best setting for having and raising children, that's correct (though currently condemned by secular society). But sometimes the term is treated as a slogan that implies that the family is a *natural* place of unity.

The book of Genesis tells us a different story. Rather than being a place of intrinsic morality and solidarity, the family is the place where many people experience betrayal, exploitation, rivalry. and a conflict over limited resources. The story of Adam and Eve and their descendants shows us that the culture originating in family life isn't the solution to the world's problems but is often the beginning of those problems.

A wise way of understanding "family values" is to see that in the family you have the opportunity to carry out an intense form of Great Commission discipleship. If parents can model wisdom and love and raise their children to deal with the temptations and challenges of family life in a godly way, the broader society will be much more easily transformed.

So if wisdom in society most easily starts in the family, where do wise families come from?

Families start with a husband and a wife. Husbands and wives start as young men and young women who are growing in wisdom … or sinking down into folly. Since Proverbs is written as advice primarily to young men, most of the material is about becoming a man who will be "husband material" and who recognizes what kind of woman would be an excellent wife. The best thing you can do to be a good husband and then a good father is to become a better man. Acquiring "proven character" (Rom. 5:4 NASB) may change the course of the future beyond anything you can imagine.

Furthermore, to get married to an excellent wife, the best you can do is become an excellent man whom such a woman would want as a husband. Other factors are largely outside your control. Proverbs indicates you should pray for her to be brought into your life, because she is hard to find (31:10). "House and wealth are inherited from fathers, but a prudent wife is from the LORD" (19:14).

I don't think this means in absolute terms that few women among all women would be good wives. Otherwise, the Bible would have to recommend that most men remain single. Rather, a man should realize that a woman who is a good match for him in particular is a special blessing.

Nor should passages about a quarrelsome wife (Prov. 21:9, 19; 25:24; 27:15) be understood as a license to become a husband who quarrels with his wife about her quarrelsome nature. That would defeat the purpose of the warnings. They are advice to a young man to be prudent in choosing whom he marries, but they are also examples to him personally of what happens if he makes life hard for those who live or work with him. Proverbs links two fools together: "A foolish son is ruin to his father, and a wife's quarreling is a continual dripping of rain" (19:13). From the perspective of Proverbs' ideal reader, a son and heir to a kingdom (1:1, 8), the first statement is more directly applicable, but the second amplifies the principle by showing that it applies in another context. If the son recognizes what trouble can be caused by a wife's quarreling, he should take heed of what damage his own quarreling can do.

The general point in Proverbs for a husband is that you should be grateful for your wife's strengths and her loyalty and that you should work on being the best husband you can be. You should train yourself to be loyal to her alone:

> Drink water from your own cistern,
>> flowing water from your own well.
> Should your springs be scattered abroad,
>> streams of water in the streets?

Let them be for yourself alone,
    and not for strangers with you.
Let your fountain be blessed,
    and rejoice in the wife of your youth,
      a lovely deer, a graceful doe.
Let her breasts fill you at all times with delight;
    be intoxicated always in her love (5:15–19).

HUSBAND MATERIAL

As mentioned earlier, Proverbs' first book and last book include material on the importance of wives. While marriage is not mentioned as much in the rest of Proverbs, this structure frames and interprets what is in view throughout the book. All Solomon's warnings against sloth and other enslaving vices, his exhortations to pursue wisdom and flee foolishness, are aimed at transforming a young man into "husband material." Not all men are called to be husbands, but the qualities a husband needs to have are good for all men.

Indeed, sloth and sexual sin seem linked. Proverbs 29:3 definitely links sexual immorality with the impoverishment that comes from slothful spending (more on that below). C. S. Lewis showed the connection when he was explaining why the habit of masturbation is bad:

> The true exercise of imagination, in my view, is (a) To help us to understand other people (b) To respond to, and, some of us, to produce art. But it has also a bad use: to provide for us, in shadowy form, a substitute for virtues, successes, distinctions etc. which ought to be sought outside in the real world — e.g., picturing all I'd do if I were rich instead of earning and saving. Masturbation involves this abuse of imagination in erotic matters (which I think bad in itself) and thereby encourages a similar abuse of it in all spheres.[11]

So pornographic images are similar to daydreaming about great wealth. "The discerning sets his face toward wisdom, but the eyes of a fool are on the ends of the earth" (Prov. 17:24).

The importance of being a good husband and father cannot be overstated. Every young man (and young woman) who is going to have children is going to become responsible for at least one future adult. While ultimately an adult is accountable for himself before God, the effect parents can have a child (and the adult the child grows into), by action or neglect, is immense. Foolish parents often have foolish children.

Growing into a wise man is the best way to prepare to become a wise spouse. To develop productive habits, like the proclivity to work, stay alert, and save money rather than be slothful, entitled, and wasteful, will have implications for what kind of husband and father you will be. There may be circumstances beyond your control that hurt your family, but you don't want to be the source of any damage to your wife or children. Growing into a wise person means providing great advantages to everyone you care for.

But there is more to becoming a worthy husband to a woman than these good habits. It will probably not shock you to read here that marriage is supposed to involve sex. Sex is how children are conceived, but that is not the reason for sex or marriage. Rather, marriage is the reason for sex. God *wanted* the human race to consist of two types of people. He wanted these two types of individuals to pair off as units. That arrangement somehow reflects God's nature and is a part of being created in God's image (Gen. 1:27). He wanted children to be raised in these families. Sex exists to encourage that bond between a man and woman, strengthen it, and be the means for God to assign children to those families.

But for sex to "work" the way it is supposed to, a certain discipline or culture should exist. Sex needs to be restricted to marriage. The more this discipline is compromised, the more vulnerable marriages and families become. Sex can't function as well as a unique bond between two people if one or both of them has engaged in it outside their relationship. You only make maturity more difficult when you engage in sex before the right context—marriage.

In his letter replying to a question about masturbation, Lewis explained how sex was meant to work in a person's life:

> For me the real evil of masturbation would be that it takes an appetite which, in lawful use, leads the individual out of himself to complete (and correct) his own personality in that of another (and finally in children and even grandchildren) and turns it back: sending the man back into the prison of himself, there to keep a harem of imaginary brides.
>
> And this harem, once admitted, works against his ever getting out and really uniting with a real woman. For the harem is always accessible, always subservient, calls for no sacrifice or adjustments, and can be endowed with erotic and psychological attractions which no real woman can rival.
>
> Among these shadowy brides he is always adored, always the perfect lover: no demand is made on his unselfishness, no mortification is ever imposed on his vanity. In the end, they become merely the medium through which he increasingly adores himself....
>
> After all, almost the *main* work of life is to *come out* of our selves, out of the little, dark prison we are all born in. Masturbation is be avoided as all things are to be avoided which retard this process. The danger is that of coming to *love* the prison.

If sex is supposed to draw you "out of yourself" to bond with another, it won't work as well if a person tries to bond with more than one. In Solomon's day, there were some legal encouragements to restrict sex to marriage, but it was never safe to assume that a man would remain celibate while single or faithful within marriage. A young man ultimately had to make sensible decisions for himself or he would suffer the consequences (along with anyone dependent on him).

Then you will understand righteousness and justice
    and equity, every good path;
for wisdom will come into your heart,
    and knowledge will be pleasant to your soul;
discretion will watch over you,
    understanding will guard you,
delivering you from the way of evil,
    from men of perverted speech....
So you will be delivered from the forbidden woman,
    from the adulteress with her smooth words (Prov. 2:9–12,
16).

Obviously, societies can help or hurt marriage through cultural norms or enforced laws, but it is a historical reality that young men must take responsibility for becoming the kind of men whom women should want to have as a lifetime companion—rather than become losers who, if they attract women at all, only attract ones who want something else. It is also a young man's responsibility to become a man who is morally capable of remaining faithful to one woman.

This means two things. First, Solomon's vision of working diligently and saving for the future also applies to sexual behavior. What Proverbs wants for young men is the ability to bring about a more glorious future—or at least to not sabotage their futures. Second, it means that, in addition to diligence and thrift, Solomon wants men to prepare for faithful marriage and for life by staying away from extra-marital sex in all its forms.

The Fantasy of Wealth: The Rich, Experienced, Wanton Wife

How Solomon confronts the temptation to adultery and fornication requires some thought. Leading up to the scenario he describes in Proverbs 7, Solomon promotes wisdom as protection against the temptations of the adulteress quite early in the book (2:16–19). Then he addresses it again in Proverbs 6:

> For the commandment is a lamp and the teaching a light,
>   and the reproofs of discipline are the way of life,
> to preserve you from the evil woman,
>   from the smooth tongue of the adulteress.
> Do not desire her beauty in your heart,
>   and do not let her capture you with her eyelashes;
> for the price of a prostitute is only a loaf of bread,
>   but a married woman hunts down a precious life (6:23–26).

Solomon knows that a prostitute, though relatively cheap compared to an adulteress, is also a forbidden woman. Solomon wants the young man to be a faithful husband (5:15–19), not a user of sex workers, which will bring a man under God's judgment (5:20–21). But the lure of the adulteress is especially powerful. As we'll see, Proverbs 7 seems like an invitation to a kind of class warfare, driven by covetousness of status and wealth along with the offer of sex.

Suppose a young man gets such offers and enjoys such dalliances. What happens when he gets too old and ugly to attract the attention of bored, rich housewives? Life without such pleasures will probably seem too drab. He will have to pay for them. And what are the chances that he'll be able to restrain himself to an affordable budget? Not good. The price of a prostitute may be "only a loaf of bread" but it will add up. "He who loves wisdom makes his father glad, but a companion of prostitutes squanders his wealth" (29:3).

In other words, the principle of dominion mentioned in Chapter 2 applies to illicit sex. As we reviewed in Chapter 2, we are made to get better at what we do. A young man who makes himself get up and start his day in a timely manner will grow better at getting up on time (and getting to bed on time). A young man who sleeps in will get "better" at oversleeping. A man who works diligently will find he becomes skilled as a worker. The man who is slothful becomes "skilled" at sloth. So also, a person who views porn or engages in worse immorality will find his life becomes more unlivable without such sinful pleasures. Rather than gaining dominion, he will be dominated.

In Proverbs 6:23–26, Solomon points out the relative risk of an adulteress compared to a prostitute to get the son to think about what he's doing, though certainly not to commend the latter option. Why be more attracted to a high-risk temptation if it is really just a desire for sex? Or is there something else involved?

Solomon's warning in Proverbs 7 is specific and detailed. He wants the young man to avoid the trap of a married, wealthy, immoral woman. He doesn't explicitly say she is older, but Solomon doesn't call her young. The impression we get is that she is older than the youth, and certainly more experienced.

And she is not tempting the young man only with sex, but with the enjoyment of wealth that is not his and he did not earn.

> I have spread my couch with coverings,
> colored linens from Egyptian linen;
> I have perfumed my bed with myrrh,
> aloes, and cinnamon. (7:16–17)

Her bed is a luxury that the youth could not afford unless he was wealthy. Her mention of the husband's "bag of money" (v. 20) that he took on his trip emphasizes the immense wealth of her household—which she is betraying. If her husband has so much money to risk going somewhere far away—a more hazardous endeavor in the ancient world—then we can safely assume he has far more wealth in his home estate.

So here is a rich woman offering a night of sinful pleasure to a young man that includes the misuse of not only the rich man's wife but also many of the husband's luxuries.

The adulterous temptress of Proverbs 7 seems unprecedented in the Bible. The closest situation, perhaps, is the story of Joseph and Potiphar's wife. But Joseph was a successful and capable manager. The wife's desires, while wrong, made more sense. She wasn't offering herself to a young stranger who hadn't accomplished anything. Joseph was a genuinely admirable man.

Perhaps the Midianite women who seduced the Hebrew men in the wilderness might be a precedent (Numbers 25), but they were doing as instructed by Midianite men (31:16).

The young man in Proverbs 7 isn't described to us in ways that lead us to believe he has worked as a faithful servant, much less been promoted as a faithful manager. Nor is there any indication of any deeper story behind the woman's seduction. The desires of the woman are left somewhat mysterious to us. Given how the story ends, we can guess that getting young men under her control has become a thrill to her.

She uses "smooth words." Paul warns against false teachers in Romans 16:18 who use smooth talk. This implies that Paul saw the woman in Proverbs 7 as a picture of a false teacher, someone having authority over a student. Indeed, she even tried to persuade the youth with a religious argument:

> I had to offer sacrifices,
>> and today I have paid my vows;
> so now I have come out to meet you,
>> to seek you eagerly and I have found you (7:14-15).

She's hinting that, because she's offered sacrifices, she's now free to cheat. That's not a credible argument for what she wants to do, but it does demonstrate that she is a false teacher. She's tempting him and telling him lies to make it easier for him to give in to the temptation.

The Bible is clear that fornication is a sin. Adultery is a sin. So what are we to make of the specifics of the situation? Why did Solomon describe this particular scenario rather than a much more common story of a young man seducing a young female? The answer is that Proverbs includes details not to obscure the evil of adultery, but to help you understand what is so tempting and what is at stake.

The key to understanding Proverbs 7 is to compare it to the temptation scenario in Proverbs 1. In both scenarios, Solomon ends by comparing these people to animals caught in a trap. In both, he tells them to avoid their path. Both are a way to death. *And both involve taking and using riches that belong to another person!*

Is Proverbs 7 warning about lusting after a beautiful woman or the lure of enjoying the luxuries that belong to others? Taking the scenario at face value, Solomon seems to think the two desires are related. Taking someone else's wife and his wealth go hand in hand.

REVIEWING THE BIG PICTURE

As we saw in Chapters 2 and 3, Solomon wants a young man to work diligently, save what he can, and trust God that in this way he will enjoy wealth that *he himself earned.* Solomon doesn't guarantee that it will be as much wealth as others have, but it will be his—and what is more, he will learn wisdom, which is more valuable than gold.

But one problem may arise, as mentioned briefly in the Introduction: As a child grows up, he sees his parents as free and himself as virtually their slave (Gal. 4:1). His parents make decisions for him, and they make their own decisions for themselves. As far as the young child is concerned, the parents are free to eat what they want, spend what they want, and go to bed when they want. A child can easily come to believe that adulthood means being free to do whatever one desires.

Hopefully, he is raised by wise parents who help him see the foolishness of that view of freedom and adulthood. The book of Proverbs might help, too.

What happens otherwise? A youth gets older and undergoes a transformation. He gets new muscles. He gets strong under the influence of a hormone-induced metamorphosis. He has new capabilities and new desires.

What does he do with them? Will he discipline himself to learn to work and save? Will he be content over the long haul—wanting to do better and working for goals, but patient with the process and trusting God for the outcome?

Or will he use his strength to rob others and take other shortcuts to get the stuff he wants right away?

Losing One's Virginity Without Losing One's Dominion

There are gangs of other young men who have decided that being a Viking or a pirate is the definition of true masculinity. Solomon says they are stupid. He says that such people become addicted to violence. They also often become attitudinally useless for any other way of life. Holding down a job and being satisfied with life becomes unthinkable for many of these people because they've trained themselves to go after big prizes that don't belong to them. They are big and strong, but they've trained themselves to remain like children who simply grab what they want.

Likewise, there's an unbelieving mentality that views the sexual temptation of Proverbs 7 as an opportunity to "become a man." But how is sex supposed to be used? Is such a use of sex particularly manly? The young man should be preparing for marriage or, if married, being loyal to his wife. In this way he will build a family as he builds his wealth—all part of building a life with his beloved.

So what is the woman actually offering the youth in Proverbs 7? Nothing but an escapist interlude where he bypasses the work and indulges in a fantasy devoid of the responsibility. Instead of being or becoming the husband of a wife who loves and respects him, he becomes a diversionary pleasure to an older woman. Rather than "becoming a man," he is led like a child by a perversion of a matriarch. He's physically an adult, but emotionally he's being transformed into a mutant overgrown child. Rather than finding a shortcut to "manhood," he is being infantilized. Rather than achieving anything, he is being trained to receive pleasure without offering anything of value.

In the legal environment in which Solomon writes, there are tremendous risks if the husband finds out, including death. But if the husband remains clueless, the youth has *still* walked into a trap. And in wayward cultures like ours, that behavior is still a path to death. Solomon's warning still applies.

The way of freedom and independence is to love one's wife and build her up and be built up by her. Just as a person who lives a life of crime becomes more useless for honest work, a man who has dalliances with strange women becomes useless at being a husband and father.

Both in the case of living by robbery and sexual immorality, a false version of adulthood and masculinity is used to lure young men into infantilism and uselessness. If a woman can capture you, then you're not ruling yourself. A young man's impatience for the rewards of life can put them out of reach, perhaps forever.

SOLOMON ON CYBERPORN

So what happens when the young man goes down a questionable street in cyberspace?

In some ways, the action is not as serious. One is not committing adultery with a woman after all.

But in other ways it is still damaging and dangerous. A young man is being infantilized by an effortless shortcut to pleasures that replace the accomplishments and responsibilities that are supposed to be associated with those pleasures. He is engaging in a fantasy rather than dealing with real life. The feelings that are supposed to be the reward of participating in life instead become available without any need to do anything meaningful. You just learn to get the satisfaction by watching videos. The viewer is getting trained in a compulsive behavior that will be a huge waste of time and get in the way of productive work.

As we've seen, C. S. Lewis warned about the abuse of the imagination in masturbation. But he wrote before the invention of the internet. Porn makes all those problems more acute and additionally undercuts one's ability to imagine. Like the rich woman who has the bed already prepared, videos don't leave a young man with anything to do. And often they lead a youth to even worse perversions than he would imagine if left to himself.

Porn is so bad that, at the time I'm writing this, non-Christians of all ages are increasingly fed up with it. The website FightTheNewDrug.org and the Reddit channel "nofap" are some of the indications that even those who have rejected biblical sexual morality realize that unending sexual fantasies and masturbation don't make them better men. Instead they become more anxious, less social, less productive, and less confident. When they break their porn habit long enough, many self-report becoming more capable, independent people. The reward of gaining dominion over their own lives increasingly outweighs the lure of porn. They feel as if they have kicked a drug.

Solomon doesn't want young men to learn to resist sexual enticements in order to rob them of happiness. He wants them to be strong, capable men who can produce wealth, handle responsibility, love their wives, and raise children.

> By wisdom a house is built,
>   and by understanding it is established;

by knowledge the rooms are filled
>with all precious and pleasant riches.
A wise man is full of strength,
>and a man of knowledge enhances his might (Prov. 24:3–5).

The satisfaction of being able to build your "house"—your life, your family—is far more substantial than the foolishness of immorality in any form.

6

KEEPING YOUR TONGUE SHEATHED, PART 1

And so it is hard to be good: for surely hard it is in each instance to find the mean, just as to find the mean point or centre of a circle is not what any man can do, but only he who knows how: just so to be angry, to give money, and be expensive, is what any man can do, and easy: but to do these to the right person, in due proportion, at the right time, with a right object, and in the right manner, this is not as before what any man can do, nor is it easy; and for this cause goodness is rare, and praiseworthy, and noble.

—Aristotle, *Nicomachean Ethics*[12]

CONTROL CHAOS, DON'T INFLAME IT

A lot of the material in the Bible dealing with speech and anger occurs together for much the same reason that, in the United States, many of the warnings about drinking irresponsibly are also about the danger of driving irresponsibly. Thus, James puts speech and anger together:

> Know this, my beloved brothers: let every person be quick to hear, slow to speak, slow to anger; for the anger of man does not produce the righteousness of God. Therefore put away all filthiness and rampant wickedness and receive with meekness the implanted word, which is able to save your souls. But be doers of the word, and not hearers only, deceiving yourselves (Jas. 1:19–22).

Notice that the progression here follows the wisdom of Proverbs. First, James says to listen rather than speak or vent your anger. Then he moves to the point of listening, which is to take action, rather than argue about it.

- "The way of a fool is right in his own eyes, but a wise man listens to advice" (Prov. 12:15).

- "The wise of heart will receive commandments, but a babbling fool will come to ruin" (Prov. 10:8).

- "A fool takes no pleasure in understanding, but only in expressing his opinion" (Prov. 18:2).

- "In all toil there is profit, but mere talk tends only to poverty" (Prov. 14:23).

As in James' letter, warnings about uncontrolled speech and uncontrolled anger often go together in Proverbs. For example, consider the following passage:

Whoever restrains his words has knowledge,

and he who has a cool spirit is a man of understanding.
Even a fool who keeps silent is considered wise;
    and when he closes his lips, he is deemed intelligent.
Whoever isolates himself seeks his own desire;
    he breaks out against all sound judgment.
A fool takes no pleasure in understanding,
    but only in expressing his opinion.
When wickedness comes, contempt comes also,
    and with dishonor comes disgrace.
The words of a man's mouth are deep waters;
    the fountain of wisdom is a bubbling brook (17:27-28; 18:1-4).

This section is unified on the issues of speech and anger as I will explain below. But let's first consider why Solomon's wisdom might seem so foreign to us on this issue. To do that it is helpful to think about the proliferation of situational comedies, or "sitcoms," on TV.

If I think about the many hours I have occupied watching sitcoms, it explains a lot about what kind of speech I have encountered (and practiced, I'm afraid) and why it has often not worked out that well for me. The essential feature of many sitcoms for every age is that someone outwits someone else. As a person encounters a situation he says something, on the spot, that is really clever. When he has an argument, he makes an off-the-cuff response that seems funny and smart, if insulting. This goes on and on.

What is true in every case in a sitcom is that no one is actually thinking up anything to say on the spot. No one spontaneously comes up with a witty comeback. It is all scripted. It was all written beforehand by a team of writers and memorized by the actors.

So a system of writing, memorization, and rehearsal is used in our culture to promote an ideal of how people should talk to one another in a quick, witty manner.

In the passage above and others, Solomon tells us that kind of speech behavior often doesn't work out in real life—not just because it's mean or gross, but because it's stupid. Intelligent human beings who want to prosper in the world cannot afford to operate their mouths that way.

In the Bible generally, having the right words for the right situation is considered very difficult. When Jesus told his disciples they would have to speak for him, he promised them supernatural aid.

> And when they bring you before the synagogues and the rulers and the authorities, do not be anxious about how you should defend yourself or what you should say, for the Holy Spirit will teach you in that very hour what you ought to say (Luke 12:11–12).

With that in mind, let's look more closely at Proverbs 17:27—18:4.

> Whoever restrains his words has knowledge,
>   and he who has a cool spirit is a man of understanding.
> Even a fool who keeps silent is considered wise;
>   when he closes his lips, he is deemed intelligent (17:27–28).

The first verse is about restraining one's speech and not making angry expressions. Verse 28 is also about speech—specifically about not doing too much of it. More on that below. But next we read:

> Whoever isolates himself seeks his own desire; he breaks out against all sound judgment. A fool takes no pleasure in understanding, but only in expressing his opinion (18:1).

Now, if I took Proverbs 18:1 by itself, one would think it referred to living by oneself. I have often looked at that verse in isolation (no pun intended) and assumed that is what it meant.

But the verse refers to hostility to "sound judgment" and the next verse says the same thing about "understanding." The warning here is that you isolate yourself when you don't listen. And one way you don't listen is by talking all the time because you don't restrain your words. If you're too in love with your own voice, you won't hear anyone else.

Then what follows is a general warning against wickedness followed by a description about how wise words can be a blessing:

> When wickedness comes, contempt comes also,
> and with dishonor comes disgrace.
> The words of a man's mouth are deep waters;
> the fountain of wisdom is a bubbling brook (18:3–4).

We'll revisit 18:4 below and see some more of what is intended by comparing the "deep waters" to the "fountain."

Looking back at the first verse (17:27), consider how Solomon describes speech. To say "Whoever restrains his words has knowledge" envisions many words inside your head trying to force their way out of your mouth. It presupposes that the key to intelligent speech is more about figuring out what not to say than about figuring what to say. The problem isn't creating the right words but restraining the many other wrong ones.

Proverbs 10:19 says the same thing: "When words are many, transgression is not lacking, but whoever restrains his lips is prudent." The picture seems to be that you have a huge supply of words, but you will do the most good and demonstrate the most intelligence and love if you release only some of them.

Why would that be the way it is for Christians? We know a bad person needs to be restrained from speaking bad words. But why should a righteous man not expect that his words will be righteous?

Revisiting the Introduction to this book, maybe you can remember learning to drive, if you are now a driver. You probably didn't have a smooth and easy experience since you had never been behind the steering wheel before. The first time you pressed the gas pedal, you probably went much faster than you meant to. The first time a new driver hits the brake, he probably stops way too fast. It can be a rather scary and jerky experience.

What's going on? A new driver is not used to having all that power under the control of the twitch of his foot. The car can go immensely fast—far faster than you need to back out of the driveway. The brakes can bring you to a stop quite quickly even if you're traveling at a great speed, far more quickly than you usually need to stop. All that power under your control, according to how hard you press on a pedal, takes some getting used to. You have to learn to restrain the power of the car. Just because the pedal will go all the way to the floorboard doesn't mean it's a good idea to push it that far.

James uses a similar analogy for speaking.

> For we all stumble in many ways. And if anyone does not stumble in what he says, he is a perfect man, able also to bridle his whole body. If we put bits into the mouths of horses so that they obey us, we guide their whole bodies as well. Look at the ships also: though they are so large and are driven by strong winds, they are guided by a very small rudder wherever the will of the pilot directs (Jas. 3:2-4).

Our words are powerful. God made us to do amazing things by speaking. For that reason, it is important to think about what we want to happen and speak according to what we want and not what makes us feel vindicated or powerful. That not only requires love towards men and obedience to God, but it also requires us to think before we speak.

And the only way we can possibly do that—the only way we will have time to think about what is the best thing to say—is if we get in the habit of hesitating to speak. Speaking slowly is a generally good habit.

Consider a well-known Proverb: "A soft answer turns away wrath, but a harsh word stirs up anger" (15:1). That is not a hard principle to figure out. It tells us that not only is the content of our reply important, but so is our tone. One reason a person might not follow that wisdom is because he doesn't care. Someone else spoke a harsh word about him and now he's mad and he's going to fight back with words, not caring about defusing the situation.

That's one kind of folly. Hopefully, you know better than that.

But even a person who is committed to loving others and being kind can become upset at how he's being spoken to and blurt out the first thing that comes into his head before he thinks about the harm it might do. Solomon is telling you that you need to get into the habit of slowing down and thinking about what you need to say. Without that habit, you're at the mercy of anyone who provokes you.

As we've already seen above, that's what James also tells us: "Know this, my beloved brothers: let every person be quick to hear, slow to speak, slow to anger" (1:19).

We are warned against angry speech, not because anger is always sinful, but because speaking while angry is so easily sinful and even self-destructive. Solomon visits the issue a lot.

- "Good sense makes one slow to anger, and it is his glory to overlook an offense" (Prov. 19:11).

- "Whoever is slow to anger has great understanding, but he who has a hasty temper exalts folly" (Prov. 14:29).

When you have been provoked, that is probably not the time to start responding off the top of your head. It is akin to driving under the influence.

A People are Known by Their Speech Habits

This may seem like rather simple advice. You might wonder why God would inspire this kind of instruction in his Word that almost seems like self-help material. But remember, God wants his people to be distinctive by the speech they are known for. Paul talks to the

Colossians about how the pagans behave and contrasts that with how Christians should behave. And, as in many other places, speech is central to the contrasting ways of life:

> In these you too once walked, when you were living in them. But now you must put them all away: anger, wrath, malice, slander, and obscene talk from your mouth. Do not lie to one another, seeing that you have put off the old self with its practices and have put on the new self, which is being renewed in knowledge after the image of its creator. Here there is not Greek and Jew, circumcised and uncircumcised, barbarian, Scythian, slave, free; but Christ is all, and in all.
>
> Put on then, as God's chosen ones, holy and beloved, compassionate hearts, kindness, humility, meekness, and patience, bearing with one another and, if one has a complaint against another, forgiving each other; as the Lord has forgiven you, so you also must forgive. And above all these put on love, which binds everything together in perfect harmony (Col. 3:7–14).

Again, becoming a person who loves God's people instead of being jealous or spiteful will do a lot, but it won't be enough. You need to *practice* the habit of being slow to speak, of restraining your words. Remember, one of the fruits of the Spirit is self-control (Gal. 5:25). Simply being a spiritual person will not guarantee everything you do will be spiritual. The fact that self-control is on the list proves that good fruit doesn't simply "flow" out of anyone. You have to exert control over your spontaneous behavior.

This is especially true of speech. You've got a powerful brain, but not everything it thinks is going to be appropriate for public consumption at any given moment. That same intelligence that can control your speech will also spontaneously supply a wide range of words for you to choose from. Which ones are best to speak out loud? You need to learn to restrain your words so you can select the right thing to say and be that fountain of wisdom. We have a lot of power at our disposal. God wants us to use our power of speech in the right way.

I wrote above about the kind of speech that is often modeled in our culture's sitcoms. We are taught to idealize a quick reply. A related assumption seems to be that we are owed the satisfaction of saying what we feel. We assume we have to "get it off our chests"—an expression that regards the desire to say words as a crushing weight. The image is that we're suffocating until we have our say.

It may be appropriate to express ourselves to a close friend or a spouse, especially if we're willing to listen to their counsel. But, in most circumstances, saying the first thing that comes to mind is more oppressive than liberating.

And let's remember the goal. The apostle Paul, speaking on another subject, spells out the goal of maturity, and defines it as self-rule—that we aren't under the power of waves and wind (Eph. 4.14). Each one of us is made in God's image, and we are supposed to take dominion over our lives. We're not going to be able to do that well if we feel obligated to speak on the basis of our feelings or thoughts at the moment and not on the basis of what we want to achieve. Solomon says that our ability to choose our spoken words and leave others unexpressed makes us greater. Restraining our words does not restrain us but empowers us.

- "Whoever is slow to anger is better than the mighty, and he who rules his spirit than he who takes a city" (Prov. 16:32).

- "A man without self-control is like a city broken into and left without walls" (Prov. 25:28).

Jesus died and rose as a new creation to reestablish us as men and women charged to take dominion over creation. As James tells us, one of the most difficult challenges is taking charge of our own speech, but it is also one of the most important for our own happiness, for our witness, and for subduing the world.

Caging Chaos Instead of Creating It

In Proverbs 18:4, Solomon uses a metaphor that refers to the story of creation: "The words of a man's mouth are deep waters; the fountain of wisdom is a bubbling brook." The context would indicate that "the fountain of wisdom" refers to wise words that nourish and refresh. But the "words of a man's mouth" are all the possible words one might say and that a foolish person might allow himself to say. Compare Proverbs 20:5, the only other reference to deep water: "The purpose in a man's heart is like deep water, but a man of understanding will draw it out."

In Genesis 1, we are told that God created heaven and earth in the beginning, but the earth was undeveloped: it was "without form and void, and darkness was over the face of the deep. And the Spirit of God was hovering over the face of the waters" (v. 2). From that point God illuminated and ordered the earth by speaking.

When Wisdom describes creation, she singles out the waters for special treatment. We've seen the passage before but we need to look at Proverbs 8:23–31 again for some details.

> Ages ago I was set up,
>> at the first, before the beginning of the earth.
> When there were no depths I was brought forth,
>> when there were no springs abounding with water.
> Before the mountains had been shaped,
>> before the hills, I was brought forth,
> before he had made the earth with its fields,
>> or the first of the dust of the world.
> When he established the heavens, I was there;
>> when he drew a circle on the face of the deep,
> when he made firm the skies above,
>> when he established the fountains of the deep,
> *when he assigned to the sea its limit,*
>> *so that the waters might not transgress his command,*
>> when he marked out the foundations of the earth,
> then I was beside him, like a master workman,
>> and I was daily his delight,

> rejoicing before him always,
>   rejoicing in his inhabited world
>   and delighting in the children of man [emphasis added].

There's only one element of creation that is given "a command." The "waters" are kept within a boundary. They are "assigned" a "limit" that they must not "transgress." We need to delve into some imagery that is used throughout the Bible to understand how this is relevant to wise speech in Proverbs.

In Genesis 1, it is possible to interpret the waters that are separated from the land on the third day to form the seas as being what is left of the original "deep." And from that point on the sea is often used as a picture of chaos that must be restrained.

> O LORD God of hosts,
>   who is mighty as you are, O LORD,
>   with your faithfulness all around you?
> You rule the raging of the sea;
>   when its waves rise, you still them.
> You crushed Rahab like a carcass;
>   you scattered your enemies with your mighty arm (Ps. 89:8–10).

"Rahab" here is a reference to Egypt as a dragon (Isa. 31:7; compare Gen. 1:21). God's defeat of Egypt at the Red Sea is often referenced as a subduing of the raging waters and a slaying of a sea monster:

> Awake, awake, put on strength,
>   O arm of the LORD;
> awake, as in days of old,
>   the generations of long ago.
> Was it not you who cut Rahab in pieces,
>   who pierced the dragon?
> Was it not you who dried up the sea,
>   the waters of the great deep,
> who made the depths of the sea a way
>   for the redeemed to pass over? (Isa. 51:9–10).

The story of God separating the sea to allow Israel to cross on dry land to escape death and slavery echoes the original story of creation. So the founding of Israel is called a kind of new creation. Thus Isaiah, again:

> I am the LORD your God,
>> who stirs up the sea so that its waves roar—
>> the LORD of hosts is his name.
> And I have put my words in your mouth
>> and covered you in the shadow of my hand,
> establishing the heavens
>> and laying the foundations of the earth,
>> and saying to Zion, 'You are my people'" (Isa. 51:15–16).

God is the maker of heaven and earth, and his establishing of his people as a nation is a comparable act of creation. Repeatedly this is described as an act of limiting the power of the sea and thereby making a habitable home on land. In many places in the Bible, the Gentile nations are identified with the chaotic sea that must be limited for the sake of the land or Israel.

> Ah, the thunder of many peoples;
>> they thunder like the thundering of the sea!
> Ah, the roar of nations;
>> they roar like the roaring of mighty waters!
> The nations roar like the roaring of many waters,
>> but he will rebuke them, and they will flee far away,
> chased like chaff on the mountains before the wind
>> and whirling dust before the storm (Isa. 17:12–13).

This isn't always a negative portrayal. For example, Isaiah describes wealth coming from these nations as if it was treasure from the sea:

> Then you shall see and be radiant;
>> your heart shall thrill and exult,
> because the abundance of the sea shall be turned to you,
>> the wealth of the nations shall come to you (Isa. 60:5).

So while the raging sea can sometimes be used as an image of the chaos of the wicked (Isa. 57:20), other times the wild and deep waters are not necessarily evil but simply uncontrolled and hazardous, even if they have future potential. This comports with the creation story in Genesis 1, which states that God made the earth in a chaotic fluid state and then brought it into order by his speech. In pagan mythologies, chaos was portrayed as an eternal reality rather than a part of creation ultimately under God's dominion.

So when Solomon says, "The words of a man's mouth are deep waters" or "The purpose in a man's heart is like deep water," he isn't necessarily referring to some deep evil in their hearts. It is true that people are sinful and wickedness can be hidden in their motives. But even without sin, people have all sorts of thoughts that, once expressed, aren't helpful to themselves or to anyone else.

If you are a young person, you probably regard yourself as intelligent. That's probably all right and not the same thing as "being wise in your own eyes," which Solomon condemns. But the smarter you are, the more connections you are able to make in your mind. You can think of many responses and associations with what's going on around you. Some of these thoughts might strike you as clever and worth sharing (so other people recognize how clever you are).

But pouring out all those "deep waters" is almost never going to be helpful. In order to be a "fountain of wisdom," you need to speak with purpose. In the words of the Apostle Paul, you need to articulate a message that is "only such as is good for building up, as fits the occasion, that it may give grace to those who hear" (Eph. 4:29). Otherwise, silence is the better option. "Even a fool who keeps silent is considered wise; when he closes his lips, he is deemed intelligent" (Prov. 17:28).

All this is true when you are feeling good. If you're angry, it becomes even more important to filter your words!

Proverbs acknowledges that a certain amount of chaos is preferable to the alternative. "Where there are no oxen, the manger is clean, but abundant crops come by the strength of the ox" (14:4). The point is to make use of the chaos and limit it from spreading beyond its useful bounds.

The challenge is to sift through our thoughts to say the right word at the right time.

- "To make an apt answer is a joy to a man, and a word in season, how good it is!" (15:23).

- "A word fitly spoken is like apples of gold in a setting of silver" (25:11).

Just as a driver has to be careful about when he presses the gas pedal, you are called to be selective about when and how you speak and what you say. God spoke order out of chaos. Humans made in God's image can speak in circumstances and have a similar effect. But they can also speak in a way that spreads chaos.

Wisdom puts a limit on chaos and you are supposed to do so as well. Often that means we need to bridle our tongues.

7

Keeping Your Tongue Sheathed, Part 2

Words—so innocent and powerless as they are, as standing in a dictionary, how potent for good and evil they become in the hands of one who knows how to combine them.

— Nathaniel Hawthorne[13]

Listening is More Important for Leadership than Speaking

In the last chapter we saw how Proverbs warns us to be slow to speak and suggests that we can and should limit chaos with our words rather than spread it. Speech is too powerful to be used carelessly.

"Death and life are in the power of the tongue," writes Solomon, "and those who love it will eat its fruits" (Prov. 18:21). He doesn't say if the fruits are healthy or poisonous. Is Solomon saying that speaking well leads to blessing, or that "all who take the sword will perish by the sword" (Matt. 26:52)? Perhaps both.

Your words are weapons, as well as medicine. Your mouth is a pistol at your hip and a shotgun over your shoulder that you are never allowed to put in a gun safe. You are armed at all times.

No one, not even the most "extreme" believer with regard to the right to bear arms, thinks that a person who shoots another should face no repercussions. Even the accidental discharge of a gun that results in no damages often leads to legal consequences. Shooting wildly in random directions is universally condemned.

There are disciplines that gun owners learn and practice in order to avoid hurting or killing anyone and causing grief to many, including themselves. Even in an area with no regulations about how firearms are stored or carried, a culture will develop among gun owners that embodies a need for caution. The rare accidental shooting teaches the rest to remain careful.

But often rhetoric about "free speech" seems to be used to defend the opposite kind of behavior—behavior that is impulsive and damaging. Because words allegedly "can't hurt you," people are not nearly as careful about what they speak or write. Often people confuse the political ideal of the right to speak without fear of government reprisal with a notion that they have a right to speak without any consequences in society.

But if you have the right to free speech, then so does everyone else. If you have the right to use abusive language, then your targets have the same right to use it against you. If you can ruin someone's reputation, that person can ruin yours.

And even if someone is supposed to recognize your right of free speech by refraining from violence against you, how do you know that they will actually show such restraint? "A fool's lips walk into a fight and his mouth invites a beating" (Prov. 18:6). Whatever your rights are in theory, Solomon wants you to think about what you are risking and what you hope to accomplish when you decide to speak or remain silent.

Also, your speech is a means by which you make agreements and put yourself under obligations (as in Prov. 6:2, referring to incurring a debt: "if you are snared in the words of your mouth, caught in the words of your mouth"). So Proverbs portrays a person who speaks too hastily as someone often lacking judgment and sales resistance.

In the last chapter we considered Proverbs 17:28, "Even a fool who keeps silent is considered wise; when he closes his lips, he is deemed intelligent." Another proverb is especially striking in comparison: "Do you see a man who is hasty in his words? There is more hope for a fool than for him" (29:20).

STARTING ARGUMENTS AND INSULTING PEOPLE IS STUPID

As we saw in the last chapter, wisdom limits chaos as much as possible. One of the major ways one can use one's words to spread chaos rather than constrain it is to start an unnecessary argument. Bickering can lead to all sorts of outcomes that you aren't able to foresee. If the "words of a man's mouth are deep waters" (Prov. 18:4), disputes that begin as a trickle can quickly become a flood. "The beginning of strife is like letting out water, so quit before the quarrel breaks out" (17:14). Proverbs warns that even bringing up a known event from the past can be a bad idea. "Whoever covers an offense seeks love, but he who repeats a matter separates close friends" (17:9).

Like any generalization, there are exceptions. There are times you might need to say something that you know others will find disagreeable. But your default attitude is supposed to be averse to controversy. That is wisdom! "It is an honor for a man to keep aloof from strife, but every fool will be quarreling" (20:3).

People often get into quarrels out of a sense of their own honor. Young men can feel as if their reputations are on the line if they don't respond to real or imagined provocations. So Solomon offers us another perspective on honor. You uphold your honor by remaining above squabbling. You should consider it beneath your dignity to get involved in arguments.

One of the problems with anger is that, if it is not restrained, it will drive you into verbal sparring. If you control your temper, not only can you restrain yourself from spreading chaos but, by example and perhaps by some well-chosen, calming words, you may also be able to help reestablish order.

- "A hot-tempered man stirs up strife, but he who is slow to anger quiets contention" (15:18).

- "The vexation of a fool is known at once, but the prudent ignores an insult" (12:16).

- "A fool gives full vent to his spirit, but a wise man quietly holds it back" (29:11).

If avoiding contention is so important, then you need to make a habit of keeping your opinion of others to yourself. Insulting people is a way to get entangled in strife. Indeed, it is best to keep to yourself what you think you know about others. You can't do as well in life if you are in the habit of causing hard feelings and creating unnecessary enemies.

> Whoever belittles his neighbor lacks sense,
> but a man of understanding remains silent.
> Whoever goes about slandering reveals secrets,
> but he who is trustworthy in spirit keeps a thing covered
> (11:12–13).

There are times to say what you know—or what you think you know—about others, but our default behavior must be restraint. Specifically, we should never reveal anything because of the thrill involved in doing so. "The words of a whisperer are like delicious morsels; they go down into the inner parts of the body" (18:8; see also 26:22).

Oddly, Proverbs 11:13 calls a person who reveals secrets a "slanderer." Even though he uses truth, the way he does so constitutes a deception. "A dishonest man spreads strife, and a whisperer separates close friends" (16:28). Telling lies and repeating truths are more or less condemned together if they are being used to cause discord.

Even forums for settling disputes should only be a last resort. It would be better to avoid such public conflicts, especially if you have not double-checked "the facts."

> What your eyes have seen
>> do not hastily bring into court,
>> for what will you do in the end,
>> when your neighbor puts you to shame?
> Argue your case with your neighbor himself,
>> and do not reveal another's secret,
> lest he who hears you bring shame upon you,
>> and your ill repute have no end (25:7b–10).

The discipline you're supposed to impose on yourself is a double standard. On the one hand, you should not provoke others. On the other hand, you must not allow yourself to be provoked. You should regard it as an honor to overlook an offense, but you should also consider it imprudent—as well as wrong in other ways—to cause an offense. If you carelessly make someone an enemy, it may change your life forever in a negative way: "A brother offended is more unyielding than a strong city, and quarreling is like the bars of a castle" (18:19).

If this strikes you as unfair, you're missing the point. There is no conflict between living in a fireproof house and adopting the habit of not starting fires in other people's houses. "For lack of wood the fire goes out, and where there is no whisperer, quarreling ceases" (26:20).

Sometimes we can feel as if the words we want to say are a fire trying to escape our lips. As Jeremiah described it, "If I say, 'I will not mention him, or speak any more in his name,' there is in my heart as it were a burning fire shut up in my bones, and I am weary with holding it in, and I cannot" (Jer. 20:9). But in that case, the fire was kindled by God's calling on Jeremiah as a prophet. Far from wanting to speak, Jeremiah knew the words he spoke would cost him dearly.

The "fire" we usually feel is kindled from another source (Jas. 3:5-6). Our desire to release it blinds us to the long-lasting regret we may suffer if we do so. One thing being "slow to speak" does for you is give you a chance to reconsider if you really need to speak, as well as what words and what tone you should use. Fire is useful, but uncontrolled blazes are a disaster.

Proverbs suggests that wise people not only don't share and repeat information about others, but also are reluctant to share their own information. "My son, be attentive to my wisdom; incline your ear to my understanding, that you may keep discretion, and your lips may guard knowledge" (Prov. 5:1-2).

Of course, any attempt to develop a habit of speaking less will involve failure. While your attempts need to be sincere, the best way to develop any habit is to keep going despite relapses. And if you're going to extend that grace to yourself, as your gracious God wants you to do, you must extend it to others. "Do not take to heart all the things that people say, lest you hear your servant cursing you. Your heart knows that many times you yourself have cursed others" (Eccl. 7:21-22).

LEAVE TOXIC TALK CULTURES

It is important to realize that one of the benefits of wisdom is "delivering you from the way of evil, from men of perverted speech" (Prov. 2:12). Such people form a culture—a culture that demonstrates to a wise observer the value of wisdom. "Wisdom rests in the heart of a man of understanding, but it makes itself known even in the midst of fools" (14:33). But the fools are busy trying to hide the obvious truth with their lies.

- "The lips of the wise spread knowledge; not so the hearts of fools" (15:7).

- "Good sense is a fountain of life to him who has it, but the instruction of fools is folly" (16:22).

This only stands to reason. If you prefer to maintain your foolish behavior rather than change it, then you will need to develop rationalizations that justify this behavior. And rationalizations work best when you can find or recruit others to agree with you.

The reason people continue to talk in ways that hurt them (and others) is because they have grown attached to the habit. It is exhilarating to belittle others; it makes you feel special. So rather than use your mind to think about what you're doing and how the results might hurt your life, you devote most of your brain power to developing excuses. You then spread these excuses to encourage the behavior in others. So those who are foolish in how they use their mouths (and in other ways) usually become sources of propaganda for folly. Inevitably, people will teach what they learn, so if they won't listen to wisdom they will teach folly. "Whoever heeds instruction is on the path to life, but he who rejects reproof leads others astray" (10:17).

Those who want to be wise will not listen to them. "An evildoer listens to wicked lips, and a liar gives ear to a mischievous tongue" (17:4).

Proverbs specifically singles out those who don't control their tempers as people to avoid hanging out with. "Make no friendship with a man given to anger, nor go with a wrathful man, lest you learn his ways and entangle yourself in a snare" (22:24–25). A "man of wrath" sounds like it might refer to a person prone to getting into fistfights. Such a person should indeed be avoided. But the term includes those who let themselves speak in anger. "A man of wrath stirs up strife, and one given to anger causes much transgression" (29:22).

People learn how to talk from others. The best way to learn to practice the speech that Proverbs recommends is to hang out with people who talk that way. The principle is also true of other kinds of behavior. "Whoever walks with the wise becomes wise, but the companion of fools will suffer harm" (13:20).

Thus, people who act foolishly often become loyal to folly, celebrate it, and revile anyone who doesn't share their love for it.

> Wisdom will come into your heart,
>> and knowledge will be pleasant to your soul;
> discretion will watch over you,
>> understanding will guard you,
> delivering you from the way of evil,
>> from men of perverted speech,
> who forsake the paths of uprightness
>> to walk in the ways of darkness,
> who rejoice in doing evil
>> and delight in the perverseness of evil,
> men whose paths are crooked,
>> and who are devious in their ways (2:10–15).

In the last chapter, we saw how Solomon believes we all have more to say than we should actually say out loud. A wise man restrains his words. With that in mind, the contrast above in Proverbs 15:7 between a wise man's *lips* and a fool's *heart* is significant: "The lips of the wise spread knowledge; not so the hearts of fools." The words don't flow from the one like they do from the other. The wise man, unlike the fool, *refrains* from spreading everything in his heart.

A little earlier Solomon writes, "The tongue of the wise commends knowledge, but the mouths of fools pour out folly" (15:2). And then, a little later, he makes even more explicit the difference between how the wise and foolish speak: "The heart of the righteous ponders how to answer, but the mouth of the wicked pours out evil things" (15:28). So while the heart of the wicked and the fool isn't worth much, it is contrasted with the tongue—not the heart—of the righteous and wise. "The tongue of the righteous is choice silver; the heart of the wicked is of little worth" (10:20).

A wise person speaks carefully and thoughtfully while a fool lets words pour out of him. "A prudent man conceals knowledge, but the heart of fools proclaims folly" (12:23). You want to be around the prudent people so you can benefit from encouragement to be slow to speak like them, rather than an irresponsible talker.

FLATTERING FAILURE

One form of speech Solomon condemns is flattery. Flattery can mean a kind of self-conscious fraud designed to make people like you by telling them what they want to hear. For example, in Psalm 78, we read:

> When he killed them, they sought him;
> they repented and sought God earnestly.
> They remembered that God was their rock,
> the Most High God their redeemer.
> But they flattered him with their mouths;
> they lied to him with their tongues.
> Their heart was not steadfast toward him;
> they were not faithful to his covenant (vv. 34–37).

This is a standard use of the word *flattery*. Rather than approaching God in sincerity, they spoke only what they thought God wanted to hear and then failed to keep their promises.

While flattery involves speech to others, it is important to remember that people also flatter themselves:

> Transgression speaks to the wicked
> deep in his heart;
> there is no fear of God
> before his eyes.

For he flatters himself in his own eyes
    that his iniquity cannot be found out and hated.
The words of his mouth are trouble and deceit;
    he has ceased to act wisely and do good (Ps. 36:1–3).

In this case, a person is saying that his behavior is fine and won't lead to disaster. He flatters himself. And if he flatters himself, we can be sure he will flatter others who act the same way, in order to encourage them to do so, and thus provide affirmation for his own practice.

Proverbs doesn't mention flattery often, but knowing this distinction helps us understand the warning in Proverbs: "A man who flatters his neighbor spreads a net for his feet. An evil man is ensnared in his transgression, but a righteous man sings and rejoices" (29:5–6). This makes the most sense if the "net" is also what "ensnared" them both. Flattery here is basically encouragement in sin or stupidity. Someone who flatters himself that his foolish behavior is good or wise will also flatter others.

A man who makes fun of a person for being restrained in speech but praises him for "telling off" someone else with unrestrained language is flattering that person in his folly. A group of boys who congratulate a peer for convincing a girl to get to a level of indecency with him are flattering him in bad behavior.

We get examples of this kind of flattery in Proverbs in the first two scenarios that Solomon describes in Proverbs 1 and 7:

"Come with us, let us lie in wait for blood;
    let us ambush the innocent without reason;
like Sheol let us swallow them alive,
    and whole, like those who go down to the pit;
we shall find all precious goods,
    we shall fill our houses with plunder;
throw in your lot among us;
    we will all have one purse" (1:11-14).

Here the youth is being told that he obviously has the ability and skills to go far. The gang leaders might want him as cannon fodder and will use him to take risks in which they will take a share of the reward. But their sales pitch is to offer him "a place on the team" as an equal.

> "I had to offer sacrifices,
>   and today I have paid my vows;
> so now I have come out to meet you,
>   to seek you eagerly, and I have found you" (Prov. 7:14–15).

The adulterous wife isn't going to admit that she thinks any youth would do. She wants the young male to feel special—like a real man—in order to get him to do what she wants and take a large risk.

Thus, Proverbs not only treats fools as sources of foolish talk, but also warns us that fools will appeal to our vanity. If someone has a conscience that is troubling him or is worried about his future prospects in light of self-sabotaging habits that he needs to break, he can probably find fools who will drown out his conscience and assure him that everything will work out. These lies, whatever the fools' conscious motives, are objectively hateful. "A lying tongue hates its victims, and a flattering mouth works ruin" (26:28).

This is important to remember in the modern world. Among the hundreds of millions of people on social media, there are bound to be quite a few who seem to be doing well despite some extreme foolishness. Those people might be thought of as models for others to follow. But even if these people's lives are as great as portrayed, they are still a tiny minority. If you follow their example, they will probably lead you to a very different outcome, as they have led many others.

Listening Well

You have probably realized by now that a major reason you should not foolishly talk is that you need to listen more to the right people, as was mentioned in the last chapter. To prefer talking to listening is to assume you already know everything important and aren't capable of being mistaken—you need no information from others. But you are not all-knowing. In order to know something, you have to first learn something.

So Proverbs devotes attention to encouraging listening and discouraging talking because it gets in the way of listening.

- "The wise of heart will receive commandments, but a babbling fool will come to ruin" (10:8).

- "By insolence comes nothing but strife, but with those who take advice is wisdom" (13:10).

- "Listen to advice and accept instruction, that you may gain wisdom in the future" (19:20).

An extreme speech habit that is designed for drowning out wisdom from others is "scoffing." Proverbs actually gives a definition of the person who is characterized by this kind of speech: "'Scoffer' is the name of the arrogant, haughty man who acts with arrogant pride" (21:24).

People engage in scoffing because it is pleasant to do so. Early on in Proverbs, Solomon attacks the habit: "How long, O simple ones, will you love being simple? How long will scoffers delight in their scoffing and fools hate knowledge?" (1:22).

Of course, to a scoffer, his reaction to the words of others seems like the way that a smart person should naturally respond to nonsense. So how do you know when you are in danger of becoming a scoffer? One way is to ask yourself if people around you are afraid to offer you advice. Do they think it would be hopeless to do so or that you would verbally attack them for doing so?

Whoever corrects a scoffer gets himself abuse,
    and he who reproves a wicked man incurs injury.
Do not reprove a scoffer, or he will hate you;
    reprove a wise man, and he will love you (9:7–8).

As you would expect, the social process mentioned above for foolish talk applies to scoffing: It gets easier if one can gather with other scoffers. Places dominated by scoffers are ruled by chaos. "Drive out a scoffer, and strife will go out, and quarreling and abuse will cease" (22:10). Scoffers are fools who are so set in their ways that they cannot be reasoned with.

Scoffers set a city aflame,
    but the wise turn away wrath.
If a wise man has an argument with a fool,
    the fool only rages and laughs, and there is no quiet (29:8–9).

While the fool rushes into nonsense and irrationality, wisdom leads in the opposite direction.

FROM SPEAKING TO THINKING

One of the common mistakes people make is to assume a wise person doesn't *need* to listen to anyone else. Scoffing, for some, becomes a way to convince oneself that one is wise. Proverbs teaches that this way of thinking is entirely backwards. "The way of a fool is right in his own eyes, but a wise man listens to advice" (12:15). A wise man doesn't want to speak too much, both because he knows speaking increases his risk of displaying stupidity and because it obstructs him from hearing what others have to say.

Another common notion about a wise man characterizes him as one who sits and thinks about issues. Solomon was a wise king and he certainly did just that. So we get proverbs like: "The one who states his case first seems right, until the other comes and examines him" (18:17). But it is a common mistake to believe you can attain wisdom by thinking hard.

That's not how it's done.

Many matters addressed in Proverbs seem pretty far from an official courtroom or throne-room situation. We've seen that over and over again. Proverbs encourages productive and peaceful habits and warns against wasteful and warring habits. Like a king choosing whom to exalt and whom to exile, every day, whether you realize it or not, you are the king of your character deciding its course.

And establishing authority over yourself to form a trustworthy character is an extremely important factor in becoming qualified to have authority over others.

In Proverbs, wisdom is for rulers, whereas folly leads to subservience. Remember, "the fool will be servant to the wise of heart" (11:29b). But there are other masters to which the fool also is a servant. Passages like "Whoever is slow to anger is better than the mighty, and he who rules his spirit than he who takes a city" (16:32) and "A man without self-control is like a city broken into and left without walls" (25:28) are two of many extolling freedom from short-term desires and impulses (e.g., 5:22–23; 6:25; 11:6; 20:25; 31:3). It is *because* he is dominated by his impulses or appetites that the fool ends up dominated by others.

So wisdom is about ruling and, therefore, judging rightly. But it applies both to ruling in a community or organization and ruling over one's self. You must rule yourself well to rule anyone else well. Otherwise, one ends up being the kind of enslaved ruler that Augustine of Hippo describes in his book, *The City of God*: "Thus, a good man, though a slave, is free; but a wicked man, though a king, is a slave. For he serves, not one man alone, but, what is worse, as many masters as he has vices."[14]

Proverbs' statements about speech, anger, and listening are especially relevant to the wisdom needed to rule others and judge their cases. For an example of how this works, consider how the virtue of patience is equated with possessing wisdom: "Whoever is slow to anger has great understanding, but he who has a hasty temper exalts folly" (14:29). If you are impatient and given to impulsive anger, you obviously lack control over yourself. Just as obviously, for that reason, you won't be able to function as a leader of others.

Likewise, if one has not developed the discipline of listening and allowing others to speak, one cannot judge a case rightly: "If one gives an answer before he hears, it is his folly and shame" (18:13). So one's personal character has to have reached some level in order to have the patience to sit in the judgment seat and the willingness to consider new information even if it doesn't line up with what you were thinking before.

The speech habits that Proverbs commends (and the speech vices that it warns against) are given to train you to be wise in your thinking. Thus, if you practice the proverb "If one gives an answer before he hears, it is his folly and shame" (18:13) over and over again until it is your automatic response, your internal thinking will likewise change. You will be a wise man who "ponders how to answer" rather than one who "pours out" words from your mouth (15:28).

So the picture of the wise man as an impartial judge and a contemplative thinker is true. But you don't get there by mental activity alone. You train your feet, hands, and tongue to allow your ears to function. By training your body, you train your mind.

If you learn to speak this way, you will not be "disarming" yourself. Solomon says just the opposite; your tongue will be a more effective weapon. "With patience a ruler may be persuaded, and a soft tongue will break a bone" (25:15).

8

BE GRATEFUL FOR YOUR KINGDOM

...If you can meet with Triumph and Disaster
And treat those two impostors just the same...

— Rudyard Kipling[15]

The wise wife is so provident and productive that "she laughs at the time to come" (Prov. 31:25). Yet in the parable of the rich fool, God condemns a man for thinking he has done well for himself by amassing supplies for the future.

> And I will say to my soul, "Soul, you have ample goods laid up for many years; relax, eat, drink, be merry." But God said to him, "Fool! This night your soul is required of you, and the things you have prepared, whose will they be?" So is the one who lays up treasure for himself and is not rich toward God (Luke 12:19–21).

Jesus' phrase for being generous to the poor—"rich toward God"—is derived from Solomon. "Whoever is generous to the poor lends to the LORD, and he will repay him for his deed" (Prov. 19:17). But there is another element to the parable that is also expounded by Solomon in another writing: the universality of death and the impossibility of controlling life:

> Again I saw that under the sun the race is not to the swift, nor the battle to the strong, nor bread to the wise, nor riches to the intelligent, nor favor to those with knowledge, but time and chance happen to them all. For man does not know his time. Like fish that are taken in an evil net, and like birds that are caught in a snare, so the children of man are snared at an evil time, when it suddenly falls upon them (Eccl. 9:11-12).

And the message in Proverbs is no different.

WISDOM IS NOT MAGIC

Many people want to accomplish things during their lives. I am not referring to items for a "bucket list," like vacationing in Rome or climbing Mount Everest. Rather, I'm referring to goals that more directly represent the "success" of a life lived wisely. These goals may be financial or more mission-oriented.

In general, thoughtful people want to acquire the financial ability to support themselves. They also want to be able to take care of their children and ensure they are well-equipped when they reach adulthood. And most people want to have some hope of taking care of themselves in their old age.

People, often when they are young, also have other kinds of aspirations. It is almost a cliche to hear some high school graduate say he wants to "change the world" or even "save the world."

Proverbs promotes wisdom by appealing to this desire to achieve some kind of success or prosperity in life.

My son, do not forget my teaching,
  but let your heart keep my commandments,
for length of days and years of life
  and peace they will add to you.
Let not steadfast love and faithfulness forsake you;
  bind them around your neck;
  write them on the tablet of your heart.
So you will find favor and good success
  in the sight of God and man (3:1–4).

Many people associate Proverbs with this passage and others like it—and interpret the book to be promising success and prosperity in the present or near-future.

But this is not how Proverbs begins. It is the violent fools who seem to have "success" in the first two chapters of Proverbs. The whole point of Wisdom is to see through the prosperity of robbers and adulteresses so you are not seduced by their offers. The reward for being wise is that you will not be included in a future "calamity," because "the upright will inherit the land" while the wicked will be evicted (2:21, 22). But this is all in the future; it isn't guaranteed to happen right away. That's why you have to use wisdom and not judge the present situation as God's final word.

Then we get language about "good success" in Proverbs 3:1–10 ending with a promise:

Honor the LORD with your wealth
  and with the firstfruits of all your produce;
then your barns will be filled with plenty,
  and your vats will be bursting with wine (3:9–10).

What follows immediately in the text after this promise seems almost contradictory. What if you've been honoring the Lord and yet find your barns contain more air than abundance and your vats are imploding rather than exploding? What's gone wrong?

Solomon's next verse seems to answer that question:

My son, do not despise the LORD's discipline

or be weary of his reproof,
for the LORD reproves him whom he loves,
    as a father the son in whom he delights (3:11–12).

So, as I've mentioned earlier, it seems that Solomon knows that wise behavior toward God and man does not guarantee material prosperity. In fact, he knows that people who act correctly are going to sometimes experience hardship that seems "unfair." So he prepares us for it by letting us know that God is strengthening us through adversity.

Somehow Proverbs has a reputation based on the first ten verses of its third chapter (along with a superficial reading of other scattered proverbs), rather than its first two chapters or much in the rest of the book.

Remember: The "discipline" and "reproof" that Solomon refers to does not imply some kind of direct correction for bad behavior. The whole point of the warnings against temptation is that Proverbs envisions a world where the righteous are enticed to copy sinners because the wicked and foolish are visibly more prosperous for a period of time. We don't live in a world where God controls our behavior by immediately rewarding or punishing every action. Rather, God changes us by challenging us. We are to prove ourselves faithful in various trials of various magnitudes, developing and demonstrating character (Jas. 1:2–4). "The crucible is for silver, and the furnace is for gold, and the LORD tests hearts" (Prov. 17:3).

WISDOM IS BETTER THAN FOLLY EVEN WHEN IT'S RISKY

Obviously, if God responded to our deeds in a quick and direct way, human beings would never become wise. Such an environment is only appropriate for very young children. But the way the world works raises the question in some people's minds: Why be wise? What is the benefit?

Some people find themselves under the power of fools, so that practicing wisdom gets them persecuted. They are punished, impoverished, and sometimes killed for being wise. To such people, Proverbs and the rest of the Bible encourage perseverance. We need to trust God that He will vindicate and reward us even after death—just as Jesus trusted and was rewarded (Heb. 12:1-10).

But what about more common circumstances where wisdom doesn't seem to reward that well? While the promises of Proverbs 3 have to be interpreted in light of chapters 1 and 2 and other Scriptures, they still have meaning. So what is that meaning?

In general, no matter how bad one's circumstances might get, you will be better off in every way by dealing with the situation wisely rather than foolishly. Wisdom may not find a way out of bad circumstances, but it will provide even material blessings for you compared to what you would receive if you embraced folly. In that context, "length of days and years of life, and peace they will add to you" is absolutely true. "Better is a poor person who walks in his integrity than one who is crooked in speech and is a fool" (Prov. 19:1).

You may or may not reach those lifelong goals by being wise, but your chances are much better if you embrace wisdom. Your actions will get you closer to your goals rather than putting more distance between you and them. Furthermore, the process will nurture your growth in wisdom, which is more precious than the goal itself (Prov. 3:15).

As I've mentioned before, if you pursue wisdom you will have the peace of knowing that you didn't sabotage your life by the bad habits you allowed to grow. Also, people who give themselves to such foolishness run the risk of hardening their hearts against God. "When a man's folly brings his way to ruin, his heart rages against the LORD" (Prov. 19:3). Yet wisdom cannot and does not guarantee that everyone will get what he wants.

Life is Vapor: Wisdom for the Riddle of Life

Many consider wisdom to be a solution to the riddle of life. They are right that life is a puzzle and that wisdom is needed to deal with life. But they are wrong that there is a "solution" to be found. Wisdom is the skill of living your life without a solution, because Proverbs is clear that no single solution exists.

- "The plans of the heart belong to man, but the answer of the tongue is from the LORD" (16:1).

- "The heart of man plans his way, but the LORD establishes his steps" (16:9).

- "Many are the plans in the mind of a man, but it is the purpose of the LORD that will stand" (19:21).

The world simply isn't under our control. We can and should live wisely and plan as best we can. But wisdom will not infallibly lead to prosperity and there are, as we have seen, plenty of rich fools. Proverbs assures us that "Better is a poor man who walks in his integrity than a rich man who is crooked in his ways" (28:6) and that "A rich man is wise in his own eyes, but a poor man who has understanding will find him out" (28:11). These proverbs indicate that wisdom does not invariably lead to wealth. They affirm that wisdom is valuable, but wisdom does not give you infallible control over life. Wisdom is acknowledging that God is in control. "A man's steps are from the LORD; how then can man understand his way?" (20:24).

Thus, Solomon wrote in Ecclesiastes:

The words of the Preacher, the son of David, king in Jerusalem.
Vapor of vapors, says the Preacher,
    vapor of vapors! All is vapor.
What does man gain by all the toil
    at which he toils under the sun?...

I have seen everything that is done under the sun, and behold, all is vapor and a striving after wind (Eccl. 1:1-3, 14 ESV, modified).

Many English translations of the Hebrew text think Solomon is talking about "vanity" or "meaninglessness" or "emptiness." But the word literally translates as "vapor" or "mist." Understanding the word as a metaphor works well with another repeated metaphor in Ecclesiastes: "striving after the wind" or "a chase after the wind" (New American Bible). Wind and vapor cannot be controlled by us. They cannot be grasped. As another writer in Proverbs asks rhetorically, "Who has gathered the wind in his fists?" (Prov. 30:4).

Consider James' application of Solomon's wisdom:

Come now, you who say, "Today or tomorrow we will go into such and such a town and spend a year there and trade and make a profit"—yet you do not know what tomorrow will bring. What is your life? For you are a mist [or "vapor"] that appears for a little time and then vanishes. Instead you ought to say, "If the Lord wills, we will live and do this or that" (Jas. 4:13–15).

In Proverbs the same word that's used in Ecclesiastes is used three times, twice by Solomon and once by King Lemuel repeating what his mother taught him:

- "Wealth gained by vapor will dwindle, but whoever gathers little by little will increase it" (13:11).

- "The getting of treasures by a lying tongue is a fleeting vapor and a snare of death" (21:6).

- "Charm is deceitful, and beauty is vapor, but a woman who fears the LORD is to be praised" (31:30).

The use of the word is slightly different in these three passages. In the last one, a woman's beauty is obviously a good gift from God, but it won't last and it won't offset bad character. So beauty can be appreciated, but a man should look for something more when he searches for a woman to marry. Relatively speaking, a woman's beauty is a mere mist.

Solomon uses the word "vapor" for a different reason in Proverbs 21:6. He says that acquiring wealth by fraud is a "fleeting vapor" as well as "a snare of death." But if good gifts from God like beauty are a vapor, why does it matter if ill-gotten gains are vaporous? The allure of fraud is that it offers a shortcut to prosperity that pretends to be guaranteed—a way to grab money out of the mist. Solomon first points out that stolen property is no more certain than any other wealth, and then points out that it comes with God's judgment, probably in this world and certainly in the next. A person who engages in fraud may think he's found a way to grasp the wind, but he is badly mistaken.

Solomon's first use of the word "vapor" in Proverbs 13:11 is a riddle. The ESV paraphrases it: "Wealth gained hastily will dwindle, but whoever gathers little by little will increase it," interpreting it as another version of Proverbs 21:5 ("The plans of the diligent lead surely to abundance, but everyone who is hasty comes only to poverty"). The justification for this translation is that Solomon is obviously contrasting whatever he means "by vapor" with gathering "little by little." Other English translators interpret the first part as "wealth gained by fraud...," perhaps thinking the message of the verse is the same as Proverbs 21:6. Whether he is referring to fraudulent schemes or not, Solomon seems to be against attempts to deal with the vaporous nature of life by some promised shortcut.

For a better understanding of the book of Ecclesiastes, I recommend *A Table in the Mist* by Jeffrey Meyers (Athanasius Press). While Proverbs commends wisdom highly, it does not preach a different message than what Ecclesiastes presents. Both books assure us that "there is more gain in wisdom than in folly, as there is more gain in light than in darkness" (Eccl. 2:13). But wisdom does not guarantee that all will be well in this life.

It is foolish to take Proverbs as a promise that you will get everything you want if you behave the right way. It is even more foolish to reject wisdom when you fail to get everything you want in life. Wisdom is of more value than what you want, and foolishness leads to death.

Proverbs teaches us to pray to God for what we truly need, which God knows better than we do:

> Two things I ask of you;
> > deny them not to me before I die:
> Remove far from me falsehood and lying;
> > give me neither poverty nor riches;
> > feed me with the food that is needful for me,
> lest I be full and deny you
> > and say, "Who is the LORD?"
> or lest I be poor and steal
> > and profane the name of my God (Prov. 30:7–9).

Both Proverbs and Ecclesiastes recommend finding joy in one's work, one's life, and (if married) one's wife:

> Go, eat your bread with joy, and drink your wine with a merry heart, for God has already approved what you do.
>
> Let your garments be always white. Let not oil be lacking on your head.
>
> Enjoy life with the wife whom you love, all the days of your vain life that he has given you under the sun, because that is your portion in life and in your toil at which you toil under the sun. Whatever your hand finds to do, do it with your might, for there is no work or thought or knowledge or wisdom in Sheol, to which you are going (Eccl. 9:7–10).

To sum up:

Ultimately, while we should strive after godly goals as we have opportunity, the wisdom we develop in pursuing those goals is more valuable than the goals themselves.

Blessed is the one who finds wisdom,
　　and the one who gets understanding,
for the gain from her is better than gain from silver
　　and her profit better than gold.
She is more precious than jewels,
　　and nothing you desire can compare with her (Prov. 3:13–
15).

God, for his part, whatever else He may want for us in this life, wants us to grow wise. "My son, if your heart is wise, my heart too will be glad" (Prov. 23:15). And he promises to give us wisdom. "If any of you lacks wisdom, let him ask God, who gives generously to all without reproach, and it will be given him" (Jas. 1:5).

One implication of the nature of the world as "vapor" is that one of the wisest things you can do is develop the habit of contentment.

GODLINESS WITH CONTENTMENT

The Apostle Paul makes a couple of statements about "godliness" in his first letter to Timothy that, at first glance, seem incompatible. They relate to Proverbs because Paul uses the term "godliness" in a way that seems virtually synonymous with what Solomon calls "wisdom." We could say wisdom means godliness especially as practiced by one who has matured. What Paul is talking about obviously overlaps with a great deal of Proverbs.

> If anyone teaches a different doctrine and does not agree with the sound words of our Lord Jesus Christ and the teaching that accords with godliness, he is puffed up with conceit and understands nothing. He has an unhealthy craving for controversy and for quarrels about words, which produce envy, dissension, slander, evil suspicions, and constant friction among people who are depraved in mind and deprived of the truth, imagining that godliness is a means of gain (1 Tim. 6:3–5).

So godliness is not a means of financial gain. At least, imagining that it is a means of gain will produce all sorts of evils—many of the same evils that Solomon encourages us to avoid. But Paul immediately adds a caveat in 1 Tim. 6:6-9. It is easy to see why: earlier he wrote to his readers that "godliness is of value in every way." Every way, including financial gain.

> Have nothing to do with irreverent, silly myths. Rather train yourself for godliness; for while bodily training is of some value, godliness is of value in every way, as it holds promise for the present life and also for the life to come (1 Tim. 4:7-8).

This passage absolutely rules out the idea that godliness is for the next life only. Paul would vehemently deny that authentic religious devotion is impractical. Unlike athletic training, godliness is useful for our lives after our deaths. But, like athletic training, godliness benefits the lives we are living now. It has benefits for the next world and for this world.

Thus, after condemning those who view godliness as "a means of gain," Paul immediately clarifies:

> But godliness with contentment is great gain, for we brought nothing into the world, and we cannot take anything out of the world. But if we have food and clothing, with these we will be content. But those who desire to be rich fall into temptation, into a snare, into many senseless and harmful desires that plunge people into ruin and destruction (1 Tim. 6:6-9).

The first premise in Paul's argument comes from another book of "wisdom literature" in the Bible—the words of Job: "Naked I came from my mother's womb, and naked shall I return. The LORD gave, and the LORD has taken away; blessed be the name of the LORD" (Job 1:21).

What Paul says after that declaration reminds us of Proverbs:

> Do not toil to acquire wealth;

> be discerning enough to desist.
> When your eyes light on it, it is gone,
>   for suddenly it sprouts wings,
>   flying like an eagle toward heaven (Prov. 23:4–5).

Wisdom knows that it is a common human condition to be dissatisfied with what you have. "Sheol and Abaddon are never satisfied, and never satisfied are the eyes of man" (Prov. 27:20). While young men are encouraged to work and save to prepare for the future, Solomon knows the unbridled drive to gain riches isn't virtuous and won't end well if permitted to run loose. But that drive seems to work for some people who haven't yet visibly suffered the results of their actions. It is easy to resent such people and yet be tempted to emulate them to get a similar level of prosperity. So Proverbs warns us:

- "A tranquil heart gives life to the flesh, but envy makes the bones rot" (14:30).

- "Let not your heart envy sinners, but continue in the fear of the LORD all the day. Surely there is a future, and your hope will not be cut off" (23:17–18).

Indeed, schemes developed by such wishful thinking and unlimited desires often distract one from productive work. "Whoever works his land will have plenty of bread, but he who follows worthless pursuits lacks sense" (12:11). These worthless pursuits would include schemes to gain wealth quickly. "A greedy man stirs up strife, but the one who trusts in the LORD will be enriched" (28:25).

Contentment may even be a helpful attitude for a lifestyle of frugal saving that Proverbs commends. It is easy to assume that a person who is content in his circumstances will not feel the need to grow a savings account or do other things to create a better future for himself. But that is mistaken. A person who is discontent with life could be driven to constantly spend to "escape" the perceived drabness of his life. He doesn't save for the future because he can't stand his current life and uses all his resources in an effort to make it more tolerable. He feels too bored to not spend. A person who is content, on the other hand, will feel less pressure to constantly purchase new things.

To put this in the language of Proverbs, godliness with contentment would mean you could live without having to often enjoy luxuries like "wine and oil" at the expense of savings (21:17). "Precious treasure and oil are in a wise man's dwelling, but a foolish man devours it" (21:20).

Likewise, pursuing future goals may seem to be the result of dissatisfaction with the present. To some extent that is probably true. But a goal worth working for usually takes a long time to reach. It is even more difficult because it is sometimes difficult to tell if one is making progress. A man hoping to win a wife and start a family or start and grow a business can't expect to follow a predictable schedule. So contentment, rather than being the enemy of pursuing long-term goals, is actually the substance of patient endurance. Rather than grow impatient and discouraged by setbacks, one keeps plodding along towards the goal. One is content to keep working diligently. "A faithful man will abound with blessings, but whoever hastens to be rich will not go unpunished" (Prov. 28:20).

Consider the parable of the prodigal son (or, rather, the two sons; Luke 15:11). The younger son was destined to inherit a large portion of his father's estate and, in the meantime, was taken care of as a son. But he couldn't be content and wait:

> And he said, "There was a man who had two sons. And the younger of them said to his father, 'Father, give me the share of property that is coming to me.' And he divided his property between them. Not many days later, the younger son gathered all he had and took a journey into a far country, and there he squandered his property in reckless living" (Luke 15:11–13).

This story is extreme but it represents what happens when a young man doesn't cultivate contentment. Barring some rare tragedy, every son is going to be present at the funeral of his father. He's not going to be a minor forever. Inevitably, he is going to be a full-grown adult. Conflicts between father and sons over how soon he gets "treated like a man" (from the son's point of view) are almost a cliche. Yet sons should realize that, at the very most, this is only a debate over timing. All too soon he will be an autonomous adult and his parents will pass on.

In the parable, it did not take long for the younger son to spend all that the father had built up and preserved for him. His impatience to be an adult made him remain perpetually a child until he had destroyed the very thing that he wanted so much. Rather than showing that he valued his inheritance by preserving or increasing it, he consumed it.

Life did not go as planned—the son didn't know about the impending famine—but the vaporous nature of life was not the main reason for his troubles. Ultimately, his lack of contentment leading to impatience caused the son to destroy his own fortune. Life is a mist. Many things do not go as we expect or want. But contentment will enable us to manage these setbacks in a productive way, and help us be cheerful and thankful even when we don't get what we want.

The son was ultimately forgiven and restored by his father. Note that it was only because the father was blessed that he was able to support his destitute son, and that blessing was partially the result of the father's wisdom. He didn't blow his fortune on "reckless living." Therefore, he could afford to slaughter a fattened calf for his son (Luke 15:23).

The vaporous nature of life means that some people will be poor and need help from others. For that reason, the vaporous nature of life doesn't mean you can afford to be unwisely wasteful. To the extent that people are obligated to help the poor, they are also obligated, if possible, to become wealthy enough to not need assistance themselves so they can help others. Folly plunders the deserving poor by spreading unnecessary poverty. Foolishness means there are fewer rich to help the poor and more poor people who need help.

I fully expect that the majority of young men who endeavor to live their lives in line with Solomon's guidance will end up being substantially more successful in life. But whether or not that happens, wisdom is of value in itself. It is a description of the character that God wants to find in men and women.

9

Training Your Hands for War

Alas! Much has been done of late to promote the production of dwarfish Christians. Poor, sickly believers turn the church into an hospital, rather than an army.

—Charles Haddon Spurgeon[16]

Blessed be the LORD, my rock,
who trains my hands for war,
and my fingers for battle;
he is my steadfast love and my fortress,
my stronghold and my deliverer,
my shield and he in whom I take refuge,
who subdues peoples under me.
— King David (*Ps. 144:1-2*).

In the last chapter I pointed out that Paul uses the term "godliness" in his first letter to Timothy in a way that seems quite close to the way that Solomon talks about Wisdom. Wisdom might be considered godliness especially as pertaining to one who has matured into adulthood.

We saw that Paul says godliness is beneficial both for this world and the next. But he says something else about godliness, too. Here's his statement again:

> Have nothing to do with irreverent, silly myths. Rather train yourself for godliness; for while bodily training is of some value, godliness is of value in every way, as it holds promise for the present life and also for the life to come (1 Tim. 4:7–8).

In his letter to Titus, Paul says something similar:

> For the grace of God has appeared, bringing salvation for all people, training us to renounce ungodliness and worldly passions, and to live self-controlled, upright, and godly lives in the present age, waiting for our blessed hope, the appearing of the glory of our great God and Savior Jesus Christ, who gave himself for us to redeem us from all lawlessness and to purify for himself a people for his own possession who are zealous for good works (Titus 2:11–14).

In context (especially Titus 2:1-10), Paul is telling Titus that older Christians should teach basic living to less mature Christians. More mature Christians are to train those around them by promoting and modeling certain practices. One accurate way to think of these practices is as moral behavior. But equally these are also skills or strengths that allow them to be productive and to achieve goals— and to create a certain kind of community and to become a certain kind of people.

Timothy is told to train himself in godliness and Titus is told that the grace of God trains everyone to "renounce ungodliness." These two commands are virtually the same. While we might be called upon to renounce ungodliness at a certain point in time, our verbal statement won't mean much unless we begin training ourselves in godly habits and breaking ungodly habits.

These two passages affirm something important: *Godliness can be trained and it should be trained!*

NOT ONLY TEACHING, BUT TRAINING

Christianity obviously presupposes that a certain kind of reality and a certain story about the past and future is true. So we can talk about what Christianity "teaches" or its doctrines (which is just another word for "teachings"). We can talk about doctrines (teachings) about the Trinity, Creation, the Fall, the Incarnation, etc. We can learn to recite the Nicene Creed as a true summary of reality and history about God and humanity. This kind of teaching is essential to Christianity. We can't trust God if we don't know whom we are trusting and what he has done for us.

But Christian teaching of that sort is simply not all that is envisioned in Scripture or in the gospel. The Great Commission spells this out for us (Matt. 28:18–20). Jesus commanded his Church to "disciple all the nations," and He dictates that it involves "teaching them to observe all that I have commanded you."

The Great Commission is our official summons to warfare on Satan's former territory. It is the fulfillment of God's commission to Joshua at the edge of the Promised Land:

> Be strong and courageous, for you shall cause this people to inherit the land that I swore to their fathers to give them. Only be strong and very courageous, being careful to do according to all the law that Moses my servant commanded you. Do not turn from it to the right hand or to the left, that you may have good success wherever you go. This Book of the Law shall not depart from your mouth, but you shall meditate on it day and night, so that you may be careful to do according to all that is written in it. For then you will make your way prosperous, and

then you will have good success. Have I not commanded you? Be strong and courageous. Do not be frightened, and do not be dismayed, for the LORD your God is with you wherever you go (Josh. 1:6-9).

That is an important story to remember when hearing the Great Commission. Christians are God's army. They are being trained as soldiers.

Of course, you can't teach others to observe all that Christ has commanded unless you remember all those commands and take steps to not let anything cause you to forget them. In doing so, the Church gets equipped for the warfare that Paul describes in his letter to the Ephesians:

For we do not wrestle against flesh and blood, but against the rulers, against the authorities, against the cosmic powers over this present darkness, against the spiritual forces of evil in the heavenly places (Eph. 6:12).

When you teach people observances, there is another word for that. You train them.

Thus Paul tells Timothy and Titus to train—train themselves and train people to train others. He tells Titus that the work of Christ was precisely to bring us into a new training regimen. Look at his words again:

For the grace of God has appeared, bringing salvation for all people, training us to renounce ungodliness and worldly passions, and to live self-controlled, upright, and godly lives in the present age... (Titus 2:11-12).

He covers the same ground in verse 14 using different words, saying that Jesus "gave himself for us to redeem us from all lawlessness and to purify for himself a people for his own possession who are zealous for good works" (Titus 2:14).

In both these statements, being trained in new behavior is treated as a kind of liberation. While someone converted to Christ will renounce sin and self-rule, Paul here says that ongoing practice is necessary. We have to be trained to renounce ungodliness and worldly passions throughout our lives in response to temptations and trials. These things happen over and over again in this present age, and we must be trained to respond to them in a way that pleases God just as often.

In verse 14, Paul elaborates that this "grace of God" that has "appeared" has redeemed us "from all lawlessness." In context, this is not talking about freedom from the punishment we deserve, but liberation from the slavery of sin as it exists in an unbelieving culture. The apostle Peter says something similar in his first letter when he writes:

> If you call on him as Father who judges impartially according to each one's deeds, conduct yourselves with fear throughout the time of your exile, knowing that *you were ransomed from the futile ways inherited from your forefathers,* not with perishable things such as silver or gold, but with the precious blood of Christ, like that of a lamb without blemish or spot (1 Pet. 1:17–19).

When Israel was in slavery in Egypt, God used the Passover Lamb to liberate them from that society and allow them to leave and become a free people. So Peter says that Jesus on the cross liberated believers from "the futile ways" in which they were held captive in a sinful culture.

In Chapter 3, we talked about Solomon's warnings against being ruled by sleep. Imagine a young man who has had to drop out of college, and also has lost several jobs, because he has a habit of sleeping in. He might even realize his behavior is self-destructive—that it is destroying his chances to succeed in life. He wants, to a certain extent, to behave better. But as far as he can tell, or anyone else who observes his life, he can't!

So this young man decides to join the military and suddenly, in a relatively short time, he learns to wake up and even be alert in the early hours of the morning. A new discipline introduced into his life suddenly frees him from his old way of life and gives him new options for his future.

Of course, it is not automatic. This young man could try to get away with as little change as possible in his new life, or he could embrace it whole-heartedly. Later in life, he could build on these better habits or neglect them. But he gets a new opportunity. If he is wise, he will make the most of it.

So Paul is advising Titus to encourage Christians to make the most of what they have been given. Christ has not only paid the penalty for sin and granted us the power of the Holy Spirit, but He has given a new pattern by which we can shape our lives so that we can break free from the warped patterns of the world. We get "to live self-controlled, upright, and godly lives in the present age" and become "zealous for good works." In that way, we get to be better soldiers in God's army.

In the middle of this description of how we are trained and ought to train ourselves, Paul mentions the goal of this work: "... waiting for our blessed hope, the appearing of the glory of our great God and Savior Jesus Christ" (Titus 2:13).

Remember Jesus' parables of the servants who are given their master's property to invest and increase for him when he returns. All our efforts in this present age, all our training to renounce ungodliness, is meant to lead us to become a people "zealous for good works." Our hope is that Jesus is going to raise us up and say to us, just as he says to the servants in the parable, "Well done, good and faithful servant. You have been faithful over little so I will set you over much" (Matt. 25:21, 23).

God loves us now, but he also wants us to change. His hope is pretty much the same as our own. That's why the Bible records prayers for deliverance where God is asked to remember his inheritance (Deut. 9:26, 29; Pss. 28:9; 74:2; 79:1-10; Isa. 63:17; Joel 2:17; Mic. 7:14). God is addressed as if he is waiting to come into *his* fortune! Amazingly, that fortune is us, transformed.

LET GO AND LET GOD?

To repeat: Godliness can be trained.

This should be cause of hope, not fear or shame. Some Christians are later converts who are immediately and drastically transformed in their behavior when they believe the gospel. Others are genuinely converted, but they obviously still struggle with bad habits from their old life. Some of those who are raised from infancy as Christians are exemplary. Others are not so much.

All four of those types of Christians share a basic mission in life: To be trained to renounce ungodliness so they become people zealous for good works. All four should improve. All four can improve. They need to be willing to be trained and to train themselves as well.

Contrast this with a common emphasis in many Evangelical circles on God miraculously implanting new desires so you do good works "naturally." What does that mean? That improved behavior will occur "automatically"? "Mechanically"?

Many people interpret Jesus' words about a tree and its fruit that way. But look at the passage in context:

> He also told them a parable: "Can a blind man lead a blind man? Will they not both fall into a pit? A disciple is not above his teacher, but everyone when he is fully trained will be like his teacher. Why do you see the speck that is in your brother's eye, but do not notice the log that is in your own eye? How can you say to your brother, 'Brother, let me take out the speck that is in your eye,' when you yourself do not see the log that is in your own eye? You hypocrite, first take the log out of your own eye, and then you will see clearly to take out the speck that is in your brother's eye.

"For no good tree bears bad fruit, nor again does a bad tree bear good fruit, for each tree is known by its own fruit. For figs are not gathered from thornbushes, nor are grapes picked from a bramble bush. The good person out of the good treasure of his heart produces good, and the evil person out of his evil treasure produces evil, for out of the abundance of the heart his mouth speaks.

"Why do you call me 'Lord, Lord,' and not do what I tell you? Everyone who comes to me and hears my words and does them, I will show you what he is like: he is like a man building a house, who dug deep and laid the foundation on the rock. And when a flood arose, the stream broke against that house and could not shake it, because it had been well built. But the one who hears and does not do them is like a man who built a house on the ground without a foundation. When the stream broke against it, immediately it fell, and the ruin of that house was great" (Luke 6:39–49).

Jesus' point is not that one automatically does good works but that one cannot claim to be a disciple unless one obeys Jesus' words. Those who want to say they are *disciples* without embracing the Lord's *discipline* are deluding themselves. "Why do you call me 'Lord, Lord,' and not do what I tell you?"

The Holy Spirit does initiate all change in us, and it is fine to experience exuberance when we are not aware of being tempted to sin. But when we face real temptation, by definition, there's nothing "natural" or "automatic" about good works. When we realize that we have habits that lead us to sin and folly, those habits have to be broken. That takes effort over ourselves.

So time and again, the Bible urges self-control in the same way and for the same reason that parents are urged to bring their young children up in the nurture and admonition of the Lord. Parents have to train their children, and all adults have to parent (and thus, train) themselves.

The Christian life is largely about destroying bad habits and cultivating good ones, not only for your own sake but so you can model this way of life for others instead of modeling something bad. As Jesus warned in Luke 6:39-40, every disciple will come to resemble his trainer, including his flaws.

So instead of dreaming of good works being mechanically produced out of our transformed hearts, often we might be better off finding ways to alter and reshape our behavior patterns.

This is basic historic Christian teaching. *The Westminster Confession*, an important Protestant document from 1649, puts it this way:

> [Believers'] ability to do good works is not at all of themselves, but wholly from the Spirit of Christ. And that they may be enabled thereunto, beside the graces they have already received, there is required an actual influence of the same Holy Spirit, to work in them to will, and to do, of His good pleasure: *yet are they not hereupon to grow negligent, as if they were not bound to perform any duty unless upon a special motion of the Spirit; but they ought to be diligent in stirring up the grace of God that is in them* (emphasis added).[17]

Be diligent!

Be diligent in finding people who will regularly show you the behavior you would like to become your own habit rather than avoiding such people out of a sense of shame. Instead of thinking of all the advantages you imagine they had in life, leading them into productive behavior, concentrate instead on how you can be more like them despite any disadvantages you imagine you have.

Also, be diligent in thinking ahead about your day and what is likely to challenge you rather than being surprised by it. Start even "pretending" more often. I mention "pretending" because of something C. S. Lewis wrote. In *Mere Christianity*, he advocated a strategy of "faking it" to stir up God's grace:

When you are not feeling particularly friendly but know you ought to be, the best thing you can do, very often, is to put on a friendly manner and behave as if you were a nicer person than you actually are. And in a few minutes, as we have all noticed, you will be really feeling friendlier than you were. Very often the only way to get a quality in reality is to start behaving as if you had it already. That is why children's games are so important. They are always pretending to be grownups—playing soldiers, playing shop. But all the time, they are hardening their muscles and sharpening their wits so that the pretence of being grown-up helps them to grow up in earnest.

Now, the moment you realise "Here I am, dressing up as Christ," it is extremely likely that you will see at once some way in which at that very moment the pretence could be made less of a pretence and more of a reality. You will find several things going on in your mind which would not be going there if you were really a son of God. Well, stop them. Or you may realize that, instead of saying your prayers, you ought to be downstairs writing a letter, or helping your wife to wash-up. Well, go and do it.[18]

That observation about children learning how to act is important. Even if the human race had never fallen into sin, they would still have to learn and change as they grew up. Luke tells us that Jesus himself increased in wisdom as he grew up (Luke 2:40, 52). But more than that, God commissioned humanity to subdue the earth. That means it was never God's plan for humans to play in a garden all day. They would have pursued various endeavors, and many of those projects would have involved cooperating with others and keeping a schedule.

That means at some point, even in a sinless world, we would have had to learn to get up in the morning and in general maintain time management. That would have taken effort and involved getting used to discomfort. In other words, we were always meant to change by training ourselves and being trained in new ways of behavior. It makes sense that in freeing us from sin, the grace of God in our lives would track with the same method of maturity that was always part of our created natures.

Total Ownership

I don't mention oversleeping to demonstrate the importance of training as a random illustration. As we have seen, it is mentioned plenty of times in the Bible in relation to the vice and folly of slothfulness. People suffer from a lack of training in this area of life all the time. The *St. Louis Sports Page* reported on Cardinals pitcher Jordan Hicks.

> It was one year ago, on Feb. 28, 2018, that Hicks decided he had to change if he wanted to be the pitcher that he and the Cardinals both knew he had the physical talent to be.
>
> That was the day when then-manager Mike Matheny told Hicks, a non-roster invitee to the Cardinals' spring camp, that he was being sent down the hall to the minor-league camp because of a problem with tardiness. It was an abrupt decision but one team management felt had to be made.
>
> It was the wake-up call Hicks admits now he needed.
>
> "I knew right then and there that something had to change," a reflective Hicks said. "'I've got to get serious.' ...
>
> "I didn't prepare. I didn't set my alarm. I didn't do the things I had to do. I just wasn't prepared."[19]

Matheny didn't send Hicks away empty-handed. He gave him a blank journal and a book entitled *Extreme Ownership*. I don't know anything about the book or its value. But the title is interesting in light of what Matheny said. He wrote a note on the book:

The note told him that I believed in him, but he needed
to take ownership of himself and his career, if he was going to
maximize his ability.... Basically telling him that the disciplines
he needed to grow as a man were the same things he needed to
allow him to succeed as an MLB level player.[20]

"Take ownership of himself." Isn't "taking ownership" a fair
paraphrase of the Dominion Mandate?

To Christians, the Bible is God's note telling us he believes in us
but we need to take ownership of ourselves and our lives if we are
going to maximize our ability.

It's worth thinking about how the failure of the disciples, as
reported in all four Gospels, is represented by the failure of Peter,
James, and John to stay awake. When Jesus told his disciples that
the Spirit was willing but the flesh was weak, it is unlikely he was
referring to their failure to have enough willpower to defy the need
for sleep. It is certainly possible that his comment was about their
failure in training themselves to sleep when they could do so and
remain awake when they were supposed to. They failed to prepare
themselves adequately for the ordeal in Jerusalem despite Jesus'
many warnings.

So they were caught sleeping when the hour of need arose.
They failed to heed the message Jesus preached earlier about
servants whom the master caught sleeping. In that area, they had
not trained themselves for godliness.

It was all right. They were still in training. Their failure at
Gethsemane was used to show them what they needed to become
and what they could become.

If you know you have to stop oversleeping, the most useless
thing you can do is hope to change your characteristic behavior the
next morning when you normally ignore your alarm. Odds are you
will just do it again. So you need to strategize to train yourself, just
like a parent would do with a son or daughter facing the same issue.
You need to make changes that will help build new habits that will
make you a person who doesn't oversleep.

If you have a duty to stir up the grace of God within you to perform a duty, then you also have a duty to train yourself to become a person who performs that duty faithfully and reliably, without hesitation—or at least with less hesitation.

God wants us to train ourselves, to dress ourselves up in godly character until it becomes second nature to us.

TRAINING IN THE "SMALL STUFF"

Though Paul compares training in godliness to athletic training, there is a major difference. There is no gym or running track for godliness. There is no time to practice apart from actual competition. Sometimes one hears of a famous person in another religion who allegedly spends the night with virgins to test his self-control, but that is not a Christian option (and it wouldn't build character anyway).

Earlier in this book (all the way back in Chapter 1) we saw that David argued he was qualified to do battle with the giant Goliath because of his work as a shepherd protecting his flock from lions and bears (1 Sam. 17:32–37). The irony here is that shepherding was a duty imposed on David because he was the youngest son. It wasn't a great honor or seen as preparation for a great task. When the prophet Samuel told Jesse to gather his sons and meet with him, Jesse didn't even bother to include David but left him with the sheep. Remember, earlier in the Bible, Jacob favored his son Joseph and thus didn't send him to shepherd the flock. He assigned his older brothers to do that work and had Joseph report on them like an overseer (Gen. 37:12-14).

David wasn't considered important and wasn't given what was considered a significant job. Yet not only did it prepare him to battle a giant, as he told Saul; it also prepared him to rule as king, as Israel celebrated in Psalm 78:

He rejected the tent of Joseph;

he did not choose the tribe of Ephraim,
but he chose the tribe of Judah,
    Mount Zion, which he loves.
He built his sanctuary like the high heavens,
    like the earth, which he has founded forever.
He chose David his servant
    and took him from the sheepfolds;
from following the nursing ewes he brought him
    to shepherd Jacob his people,
    Israel his inheritance.
With upright heart he shepherded them
    and guided them with his skillful hand (Ps. 78:67–72).

So when life seems aggravatingly trivial, don't increase your dissatisfaction by imagining yourself excelling at "better things." Pray for better things, but deal with the aggravations as you think God would do if he were in your place. Learn and show wisdom in your present circumstances so that God might decide you're capable of honoring him in "more important" matters. "Do you see a man skillful in his work? He will stand before kings; he will not stand before obscure men" (Prov. 22:29).

We all stand before God. If we can't convince ourselves that what is going on in our lives right now is that important, we should at least remind ourselves that it is an opportunity to train in wisdom for some future situation God will give us.

People in worse situations than most of us, with dimmer prospects for their earthly future, have been called to this kind of wisdom:

> Slaves, obey your earthly masters with fear and trembling, with a sincere heart, as you would Christ, not by the way of eye-service, as people-pleasers, but as slaves of Christ, doing the will of God from the heart, rendering service with a good will as to the Lord and not to man, knowing that whatever good anyone does, this he will receive back from the Lord, whether he is a slave or is free (Eph. 6:5–8).

There is an observation ascribed to G. K. Chesterton that goes as follows: "Man seems to be capable of great virtues but not of small virtues; capable of defying his torturer but not of keeping his temper."[21] But is this really accurate? We hear about heroic actions in harsh situation because they stand out. But we don't hear that often of those who fail to show those "great virtues." Maybe, if more people trained themselves to keep their tempers, we would find many more displays of heroism in harsh situations.

Blaise Pascal, a French writer and theologian, once wrote, "A man's virtue should not be measured by his occasional exertions, but by his ordinary doings."[22] This sounds agreeable with the Apostle Paul's exhortations to Christians to remain faithful in daily Christian life. His attention to our "ordinary doings" sounds like it might make our "occasional exertions" more powerful.

To put it another way, Christian young men are often exhorted to "do hard things." But people can't do hard things often or well or with predictable success, because that's just what "hard" *means*. But if you want to do hard things often, well, and successfully, you have to train yourself until they feel (relatively) easy. "Train yourself for godliness..."

While one should never use one's lack of training as an excuse to sin, since neglecting such training is also a sin, Christian behavior is ideally done by a kind of "muscle memory." Holy living can be stalled by inappropriate demands for mindfulness of God's glory, gratitude, etc. Imagine teaching someone to drive by mandating certain thoughts or attitudes be present with each use of the gas pedal or the brake. That would likely get the person involved in a traffic accident!

Some even turn the truth that we should act from proper motives into a principle that unless you have the proper motives, you shouldn't do the act. If you're not washing the dishes out of love but are doing it only because they're dirty or because it's your chore or because you've been told to or whatever, that's not true obedience. In fact, some might say, you're a hypocrite if you do what God tells you—especially worship—without having completely pure motives.

But we have to obey and get our hearts in order along the way. Sometimes the act comes first. And acting as a husband should act, even when you don't feel like it, is not hypocrisy; it's being who you are. So too, it's not hypocrisy to pray when you don't feel like it, because that's the right behavior for who you are as God's child, no matter how you feel at the moment.

If you realize that your attitude is deficient, you should work on it and pray about it. But you shouldn't use it as an excuse to exempt yourself from doing your duty. Problems in your attitude or motives will likely produce flaws in your obedience—you are hesitant or tend to grumble—and so your goal should be to perform better rather than cease to perform until your attitude is right.

Going back to the Bible's use of oversleeping as an analogy for sloth and folly, think of how the people who have trained themselves to get up in the morning experience their alarm clock blaring in their ears. Do they groan and hit the snooze button? No. They get up. If they're especially tired they might groan, but they usually don't even consider the option of sleeping longer. If they think anything about it they resolve to get to bed earlier or get a nap when possible. They don't struggle as those untrained in awaking on a schedule struggle.

The Apostle John writes, "For this is the love of God, that we keep his commandments. And his commandments are not burdensome" (1 John 5:3). And for those who learned the wisdom of "love not sleep" (Prov. 20:13), the alarm clock is not burdensome.

They have become stronger in the daily warfare by being trained.

◊

We are disciples, so we must submit to the discipline of the Lord, for his yoke is easy and his burden is light. We are soldiers that God has recruited into his army, so we must allow him to train our fingers for battle.

We must subdue ourselves under God's command so we can sing more clearly Psalm 18:34: "He trains my hands for war, so that my arms can bend a bow of bronze."

Epilogue:

Your Kingdom Awaits

Youth is the golden period of life, and every well-spent moment
will be like good seed planted in an auspicious season.
— Eliza Cook[23]

There is a saying, commonly referred to as an "old Chinese proverb," that the best time to plant a tree is twenty years ago and the second best time is today. When it comes to seeking wisdom, the two points in time are closer together the younger you are. If you're a young man, you're near the optimal moment.

Seeking wisdom is the duty of all Christians of every age and station in life, but it is especially important for those who become aware of this duty in their youth. Start now and become a more faithful, reliable, capable adult. For what it's worth, you will probably be a much happier person.

Go back to the example of oversleeping we revisited in the last chapter: If one learns to wake up on time to get things done as a sixteen-year-old, one will be far more productive during the next decade than someone who learns to do it at the age of twenty-six. I'm not referring to the monetary income from being a reliable worker for a longer period of time. That may be significant in some cases, but there are other issues. If a person is sleeping away hours of his life—or, what is the same thing, staying up late partying or playing video games—he is missing an opportunity to work on himself in other areas.

It is possible to be wise in various ways, yet foolish in one area. But it is more common for foolishness to spread. A person who oversleeps because he's staying out too late, will likely try to earn just enough money to finance his late-night recreations because anything more would cost him some of those recreations. Each time he has an emergency he will be forced to beg for help or go into debt. Working on developing wisdom in areas relating to diligent labor or savings will not even be on his radar. In this way, one behavioral problem prevents him from even thinking about developing any productive habits.

And what about the person who still has a problem with sleep when he's thirty-six years old? By that time, he has probably realized how much his bad habit has cost him. For just that reason, he may be more resistant to changing his behavior. If he simply imposes some disciplines on himself to break the bad habit and develop a better one then he would have to acknowledge the fact that he has robbed himself for decades, along with anyone who depends on him. Many people would rather believe they're the victims of a genetic disorder that keeps them asleep than believe they cost themselves so much by living passively with regard to their bad habit.

When you continue in a habit for a long time, it usually gets harder to break. In fact, the habit seems normal and people without that habit seem strange. For that reason alone, the younger you are, the greater the opportunity you have to avoid bad habits and build good ones.

Obviously, people at all ages, when they finally listen to the claims of wisdom, will be better off if they begin the work to rid themselves of foolishness. Starting later will make the process more difficult, and a person will have more regrets to deal with. Yet being discouraged by past foolishness is no reason to continue in it. It is irrational to waste time thinking about how much time you have wasted. The proper and reasonable response is to get busy with what time you have remaining! But it is easy to allow discouragement to kill your motivation to escape foolishness.

If you are young, you have a chance to avoid all that self-inflicted loss of confidence.

BUILDING A BETTER MAN

To consider all this another way, we know that parents who are wise and conscientious can train children so they can be more productive and effective adults. "Train up a child in the way he should go; even when he is old he will not depart from it" (Prov. 22:6). But if it is to a person's benefit to be parented wisely and faithfully, it is also to his benefit to be thankful for his parents' work and to be cooperative with them rather than resistant and resentful. He will be better off if he has a wise attitude towards his parents early in his life rather than realizing their value later.

Wise Christian parents raise their children with a goal in view: to equip them to become wise Christian adults. At first, a child is too immature to imagine that outcome. It doesn't seem real to him, and he doesn't know enough to even imagine what "being grown up" would be like. But as he grows that changes, partly because he gets closer to adulthood and partly because he sees how he is unlike the younger child he once was. He realizes that he is changing and can partially extrapolate what changes lie ahead. At that point, the child (or young man) starts to actively help or hinder his godly parents in their project of training him to be a better man.

"When I was a child, I spoke like a child, I thought like a child, I reasoned like a child. When I became a man, I gave up childish ways," writes the Apostle Paul (1 Cor. 13:11). Being a child is fine for a child, but if you are starting to think about your future—what you will do, how you will live, who you will become—then you are on the threshold of adulthood. It's time to intentionally work towards wisdom. You will never have this opportunity again.

Whether you realize it or not, what you are doing when you are young is building the man you will be. Build according to God's blueprint from the start! An adult can repent, but he has the added hardship of having to demolish what he built wrong—to break his foolish habits as well as adopt wiser behaviors. How much better to start before you have had a chance to develop a flawed character!

You are only young once. Pursue wisdom now. Don't wait.

> Get wisdom; get insight;
> > do not forget, and do not turn away from the words of my
> mouth.
> Do not forsake her, and she will keep you;
> > love her, and she will guard you.
> The beginning of wisdom is this: Get wisdom,
> > and whatever you get, get insight.
> Prize her highly, and she will exalt you;
> > she will honor you if you embrace her.
> She will place on your head a graceful garland;
> > she will bestow on you a beautiful crown (Prov. 4:5–9).

ENDNOTES

1   Jean-Jacques Rousseau, "The Social Contract," in *The Social Contract and Other Later Political Writings*, Cambridge Texts in the History of Political Thought, trans. Victor Gourevitch (Cambridge: Cambridge University Press, 1997), 41.]

2   Frank Herbert, *Chapterhouse: Dune* (New York: Ace, 1985; reprint, 2009), 481.

3   J. R. R. Tolkien, *The Lord of the Rings: The Fellowship of the Ring* (1954, 1955; reprint, Boston: Houghton Mifflin, 2004), 170.

4   C. H. Spurgeon, "The Minister's Self-Watch," *Lectures to My Students* (Grand Rapids: Zondervan, 1954), 7–8.

5   Albert Jack Nock, "Our Enemy, the State" Foundation for Economic Education (The full text of Nock's 1935 book was republished online by the Foundation for Economic Education), https://fee.org/resources/our-enemy-the-state/

6   Cornelius Van Til, In Defense of the Faith, Vol. III, Christian Theistic Ethics (Philadelphia: den Dulk Christian Foundation, 1974).

7   Rudyard Kipling, "If," Poetry Foundation, 1943, https://www.poetryfoundation.org/poems/46473/if---.

8   Benjamin Franklin, "Poor Richard Improved," The Library of America, 1758, https://usa.usembassy.de/etexts/funddocs/loa/bf1758.htm.

9   C.S. Lewis, "Man or Rabbit?,"*God in the Dock* (reprint, Grand Rapids: Eerdmans, 2014), 111-112.

10   Homer, *The Odyssey*, trans. Richmond Lattimore (New York: Harper & Row, Publishers Inc., 1965), Book VI, lines 182-184.

11   C.S. Lewis, *Yours, Jack: Spiritual Direction from C. S. Lewis* (New York: HarperCollins, 2008), 292–293.

12   Aristotle, *Nicomachean Ethics*, Book 2, Chapter 9 (Project Gutenberg, 2005), https://www.gutenberg.org/files/8438/8438-h/8438-h.htm#link2H_4_0004.

13   Nathaniel Hawthorne, *First Editions of Works of Nathaniel Hawthorne and Others*, Part II (Boston 1906), 690.

14   Augustine, *The City of God*, Books I–VII, trans. Demetrius B. Zema and Gerald G. Walsh, The Fathers of the Church (1950; reprint, Washington, DC: Catholic University of America Press, 2008), 194.

15   Rudyard Kipling, "If," Poetry Foundation, 1943, https://www.poetryfoundation.org/poems/46473/if---.

16   Charles H. Spurgeon, "Foundation work #2094," a sermon delivered at Metropolitan Tabernacle in Newington, Spurgeon Gems, https://www.spurgeongems.org/sermon/chs2094.pdf.

17   Macpherson, John. n.d. *The Westminster Confession of Faith*, 16.3 (Edinburgh: T. & T. Clark, 1881), 106.

18   C.S. Lewis, *Mere Christianity* (reprint, San Francisco: HarperOne, 2015), 188–189.

19   Rob Rains, "Anniversary of wake-up call will pass quietly for Cardinals' Jordan Hicks, who knew 'something had to change,'"STLSportspage.com, February 27, 2019, https://stlsportspage.com/2019/02/27/anniversary-of-wake-up-call-will-pass-quietly-for-cardinals-jordan-hicks-who-knew-something-had-to-change/.

20   Ibid.

21   G.K. Chesterton, The Autobiography of G. K. Chesterton (1936; reprint, San Francisco: Ignatius Press, 2006), 239.

22   Blaise Pascal, *Thoughts on Religion and Other Subjects*, trans. Rev. Edward Craig (Amherst, Massachussetts: J.S. & C. Adams, 1829), 270.

23   Eliza Cook, *Eliza Cook's Journal*, Volume 2 (London: John Owen Clarke, 1850), 32).

CPSIA information can be obtained
at www.ICGtesting.com
Printed in the USA
LVHW010154121020
668551LV00016B/649

9 781733 535670